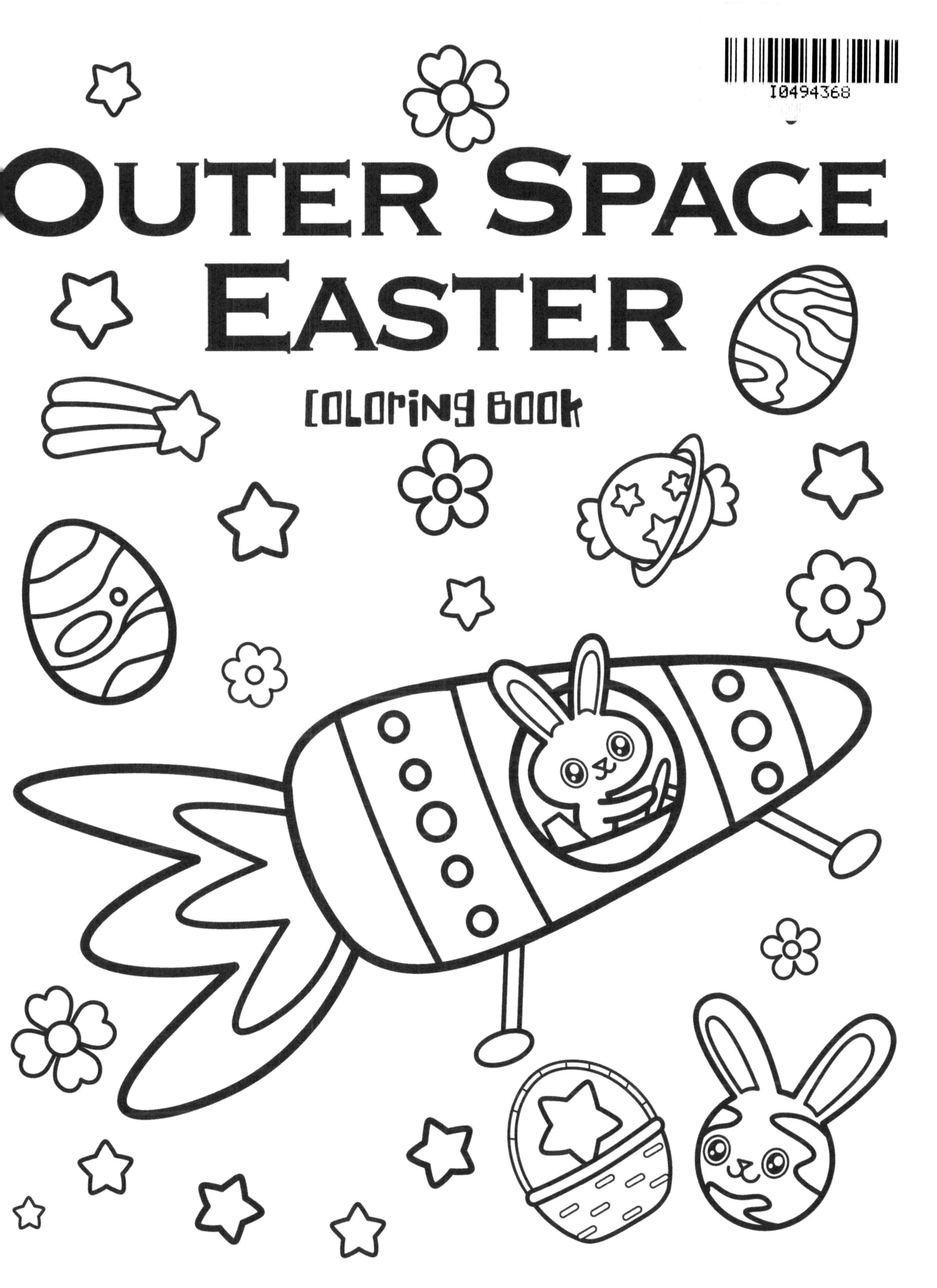

OUTER SPACE EASTER

COLORING BOOK

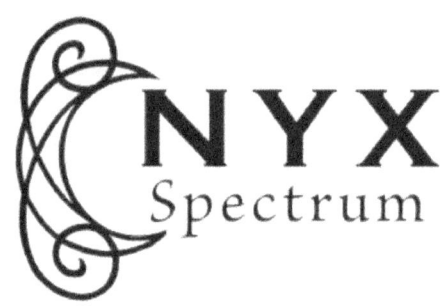

Thank you for purchasing one of our Coloring Books!

If you loved this coloring book we would like to give you an exclusive offer!
Subscribe to our email today and receive trendy Free Coloring Pages not found in any of our books.

We will also update you on our New and Upcoming Coloring Books, only found on Amazon.com!
Email us at nyxspectrum@gmail.com or visit our website: www.nyxspectrum.com

Published in 2019 by
Nyx Spectrum

Printed in the United States of America

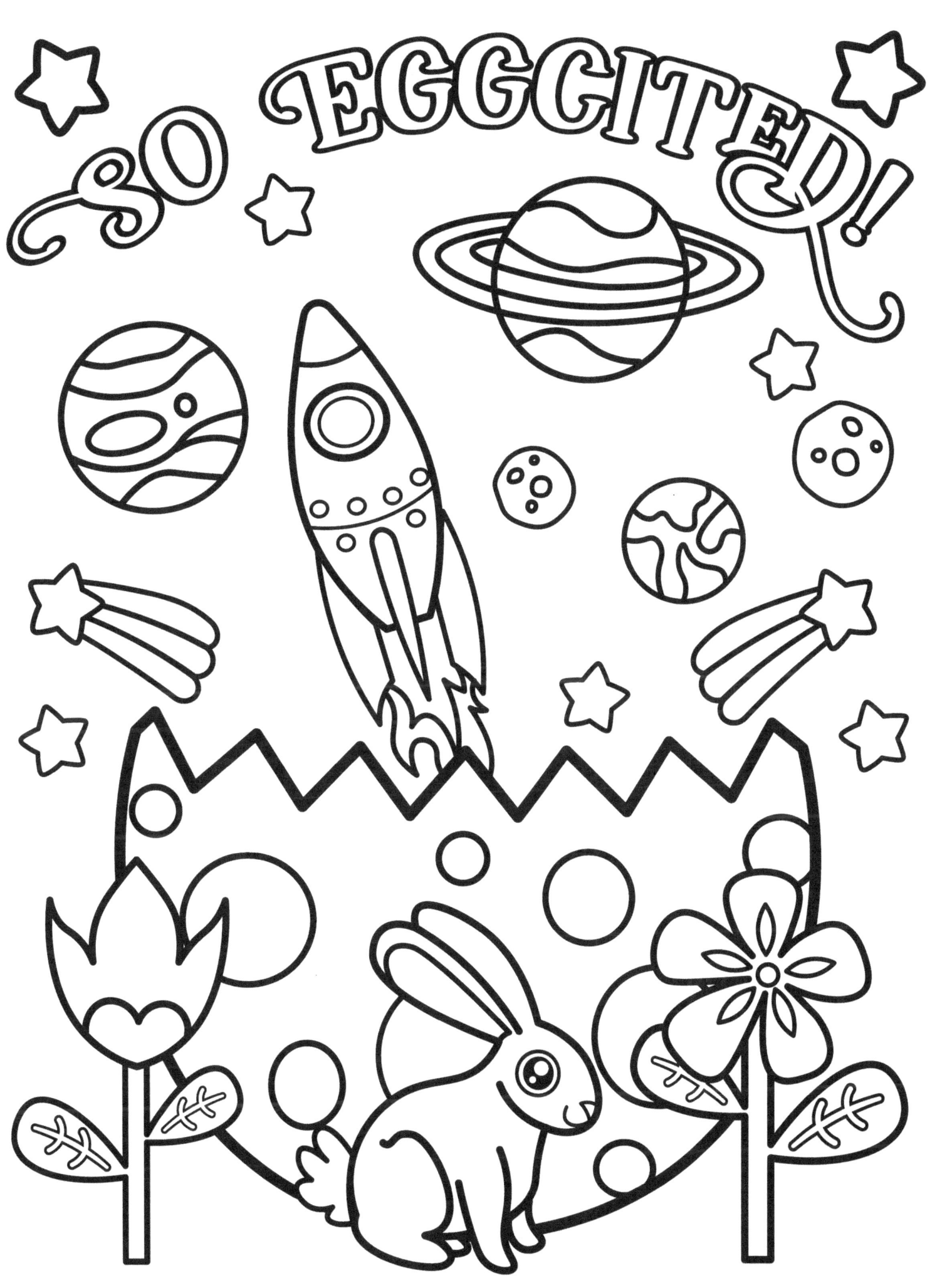

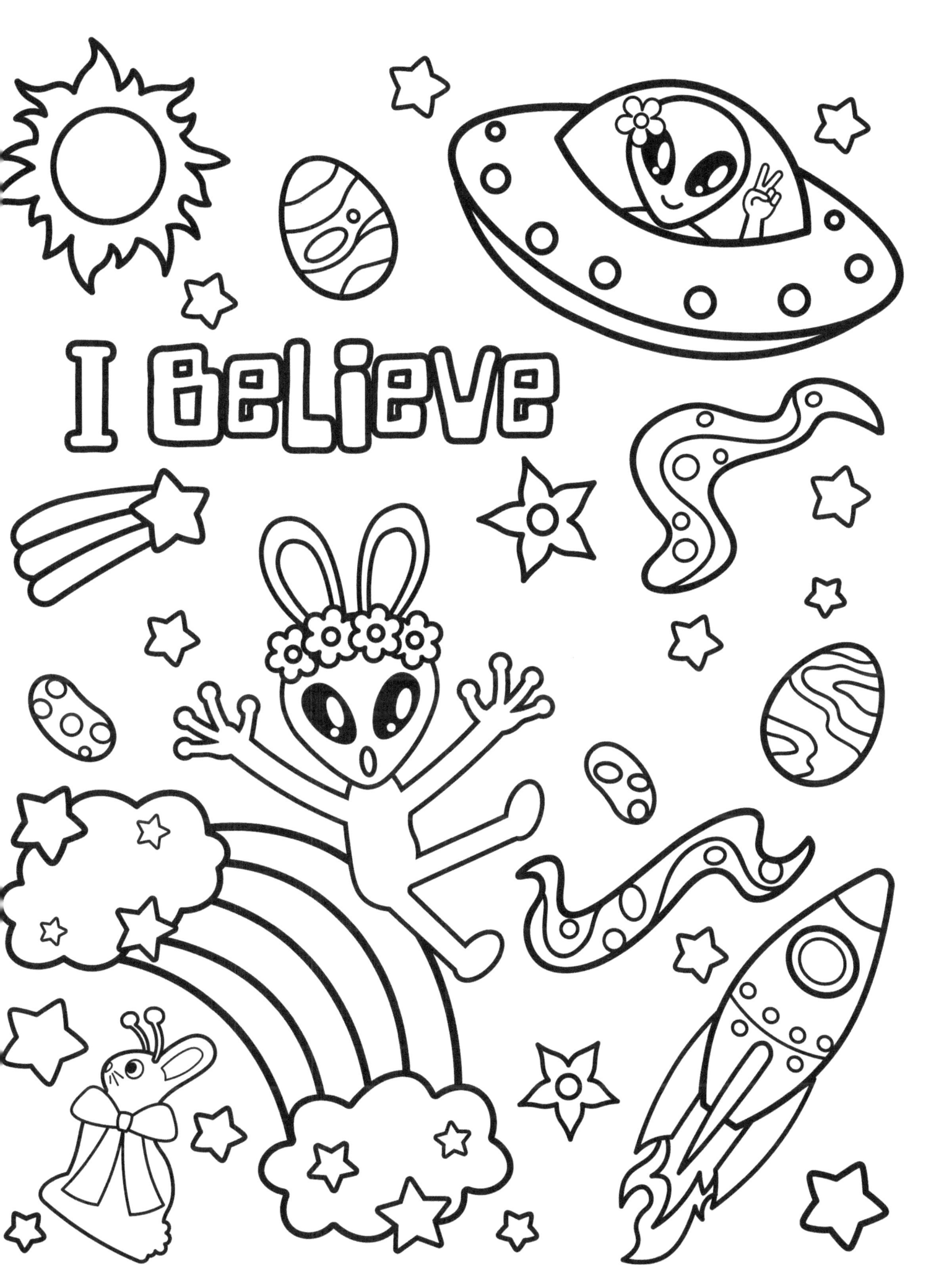

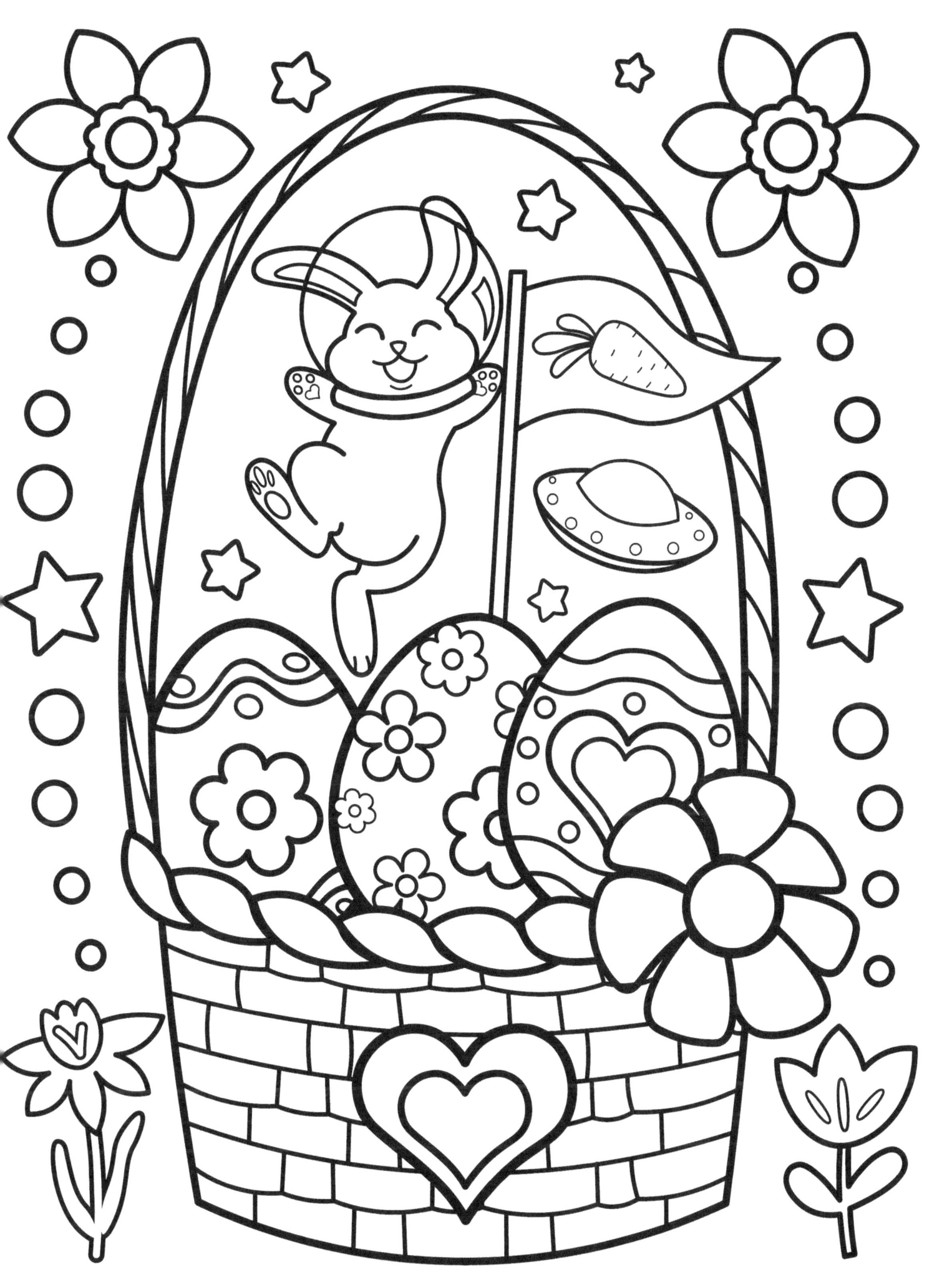

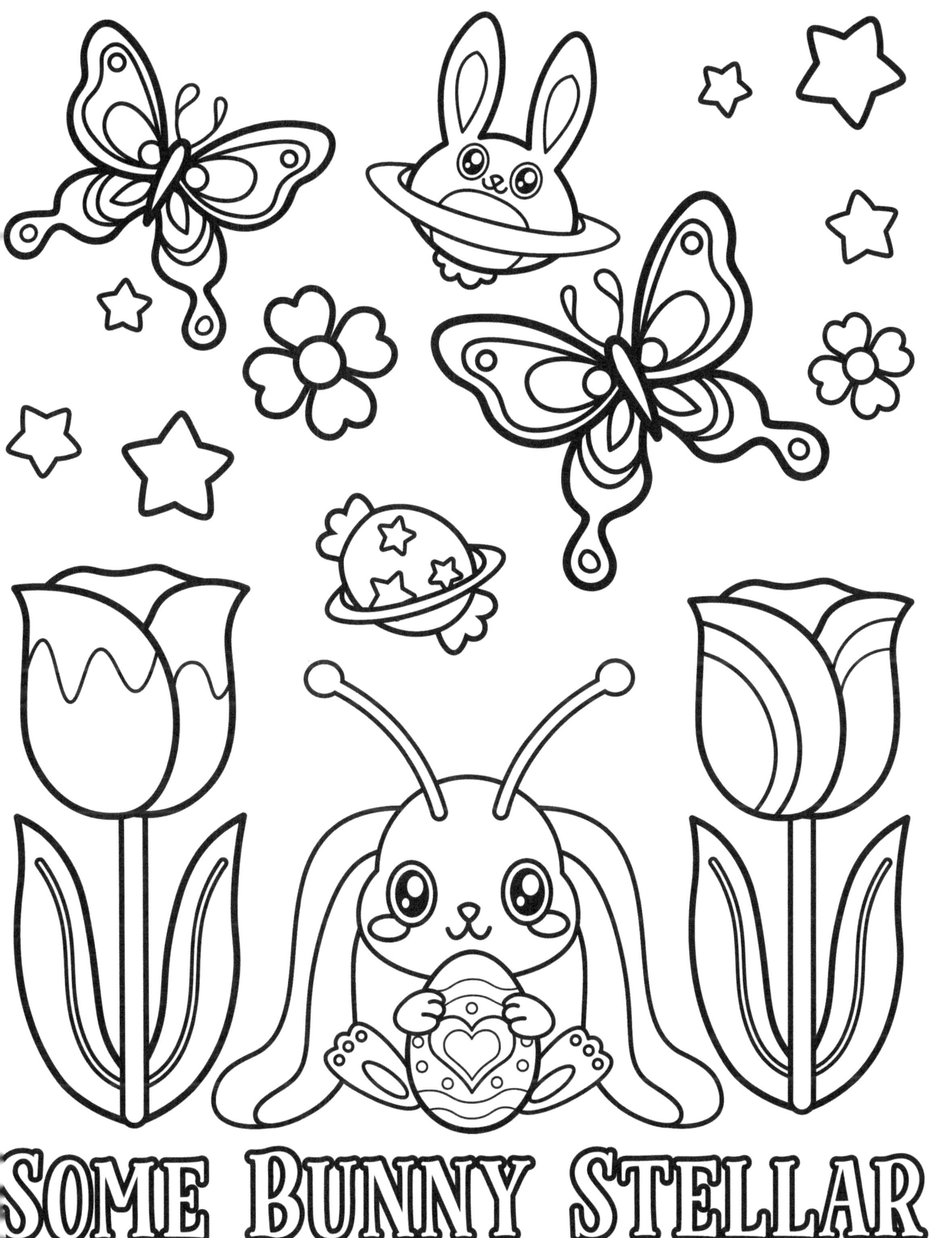

SOME BUNNY STELLAR

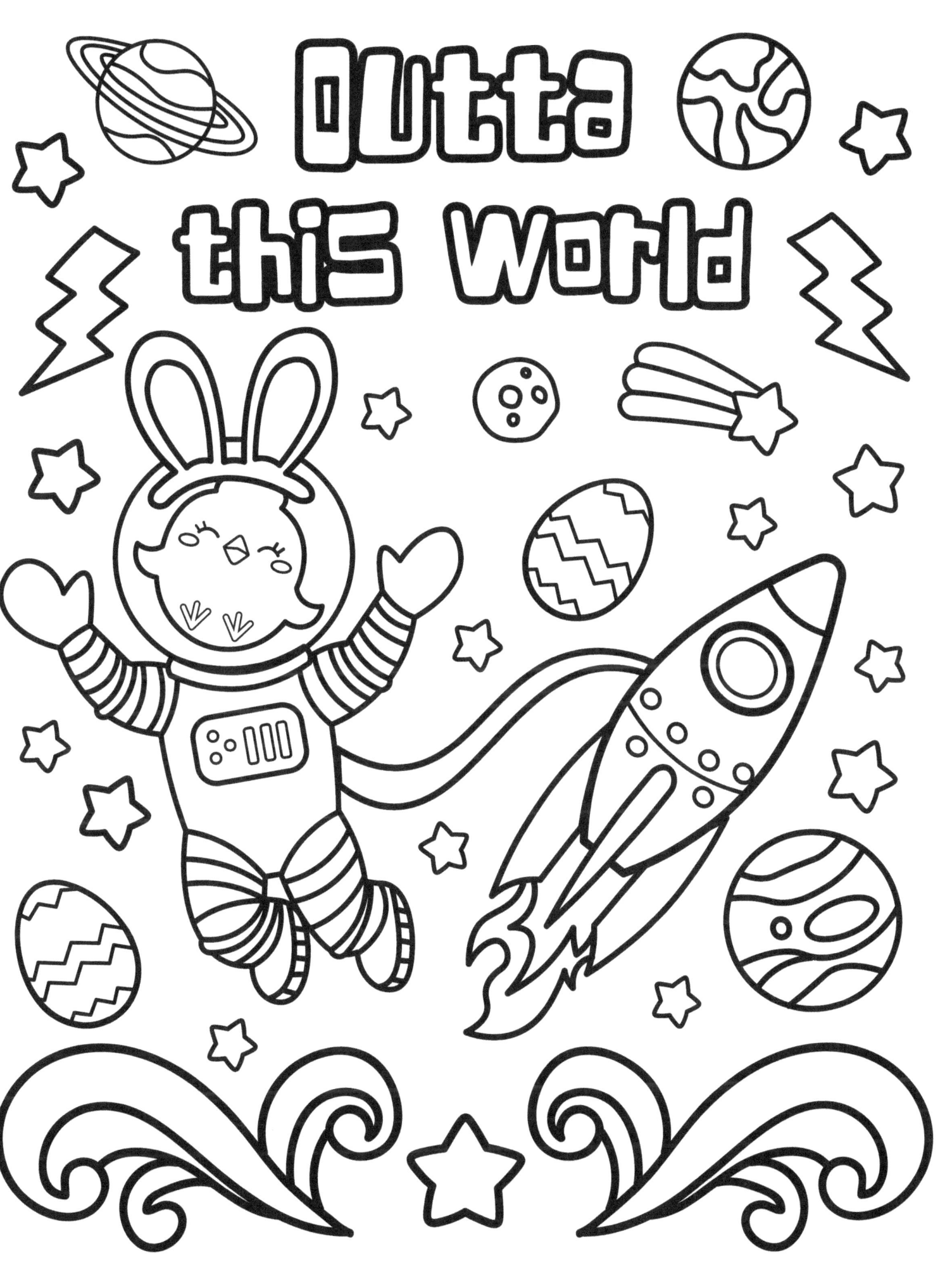

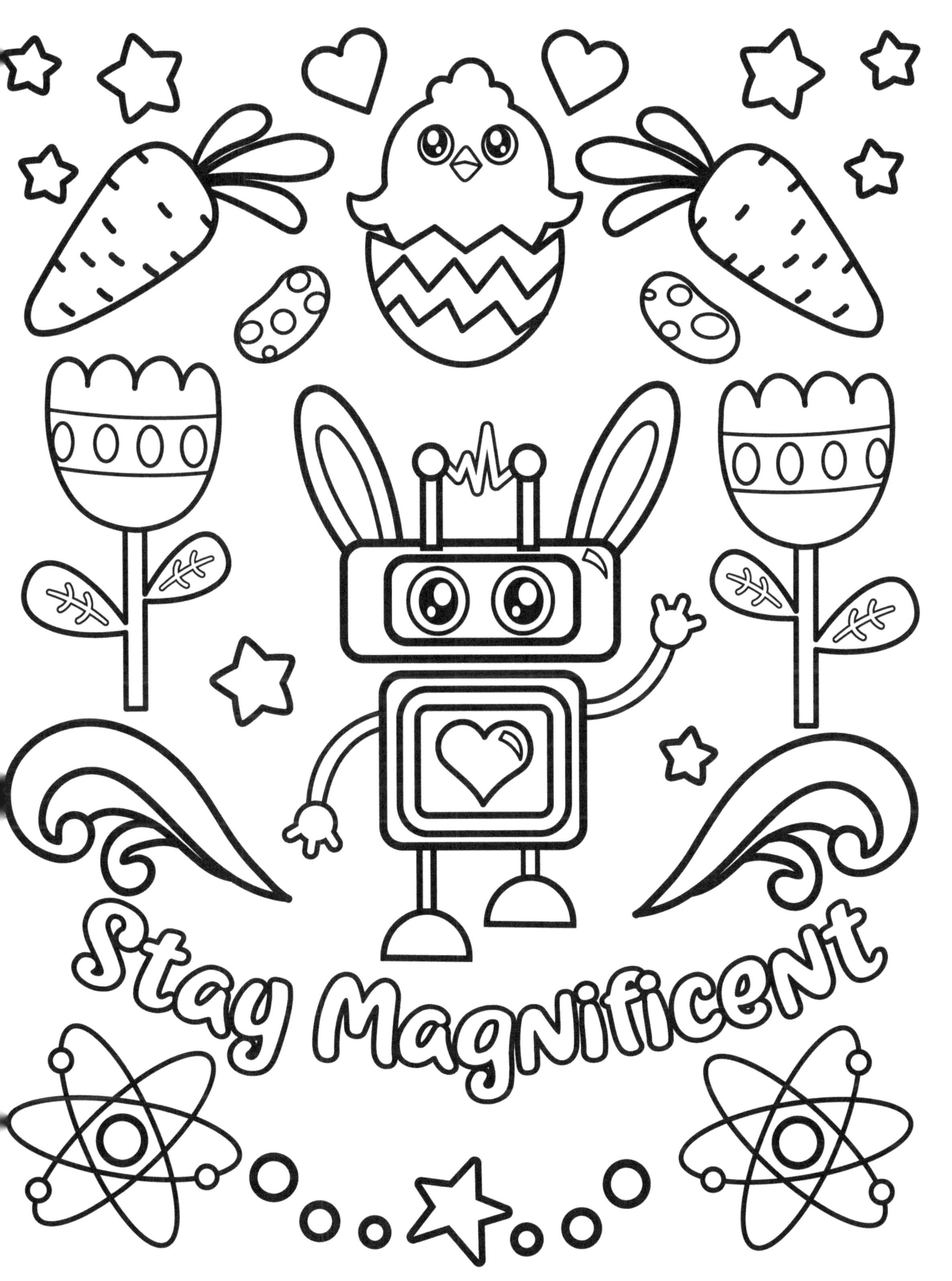

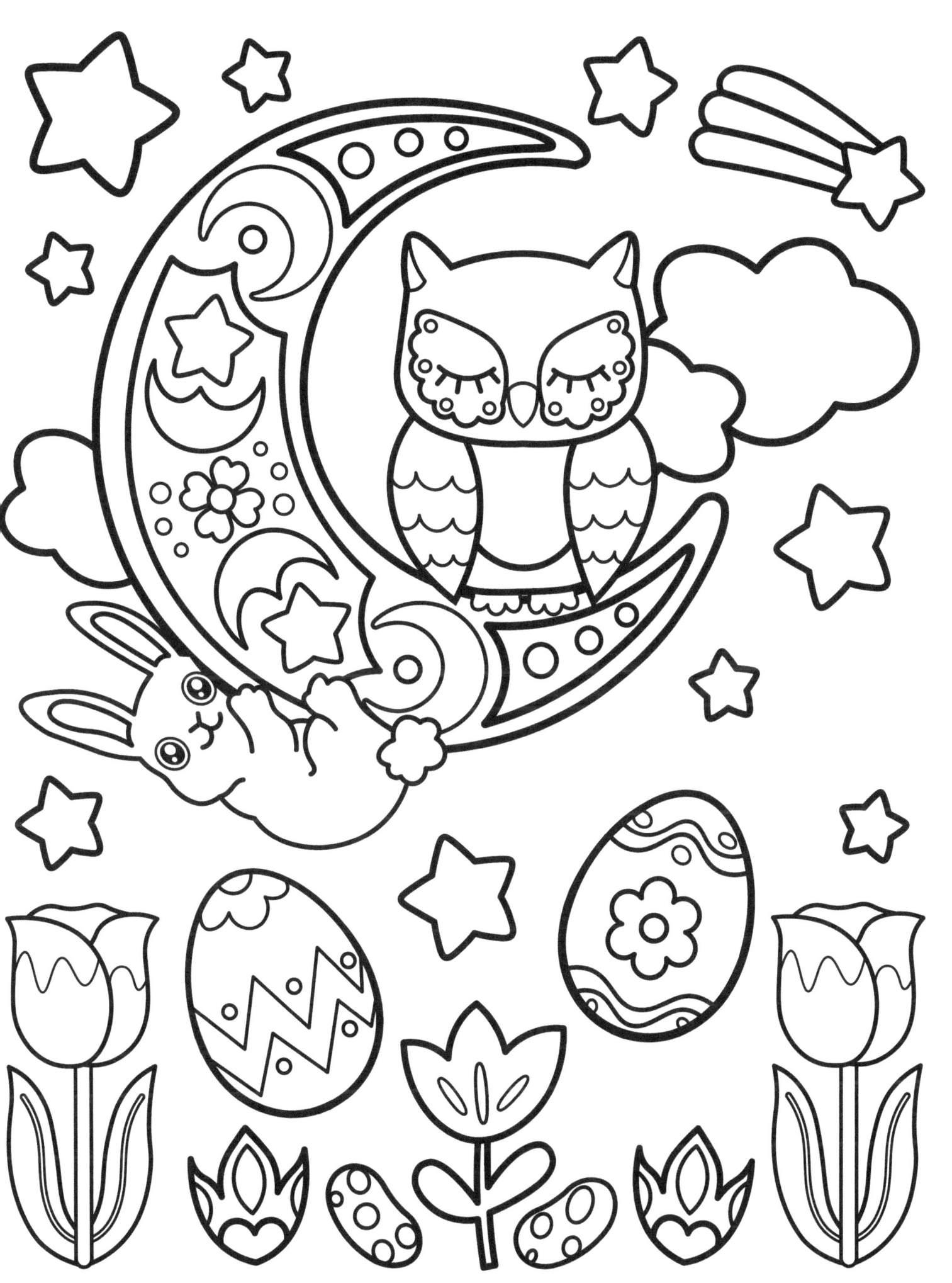

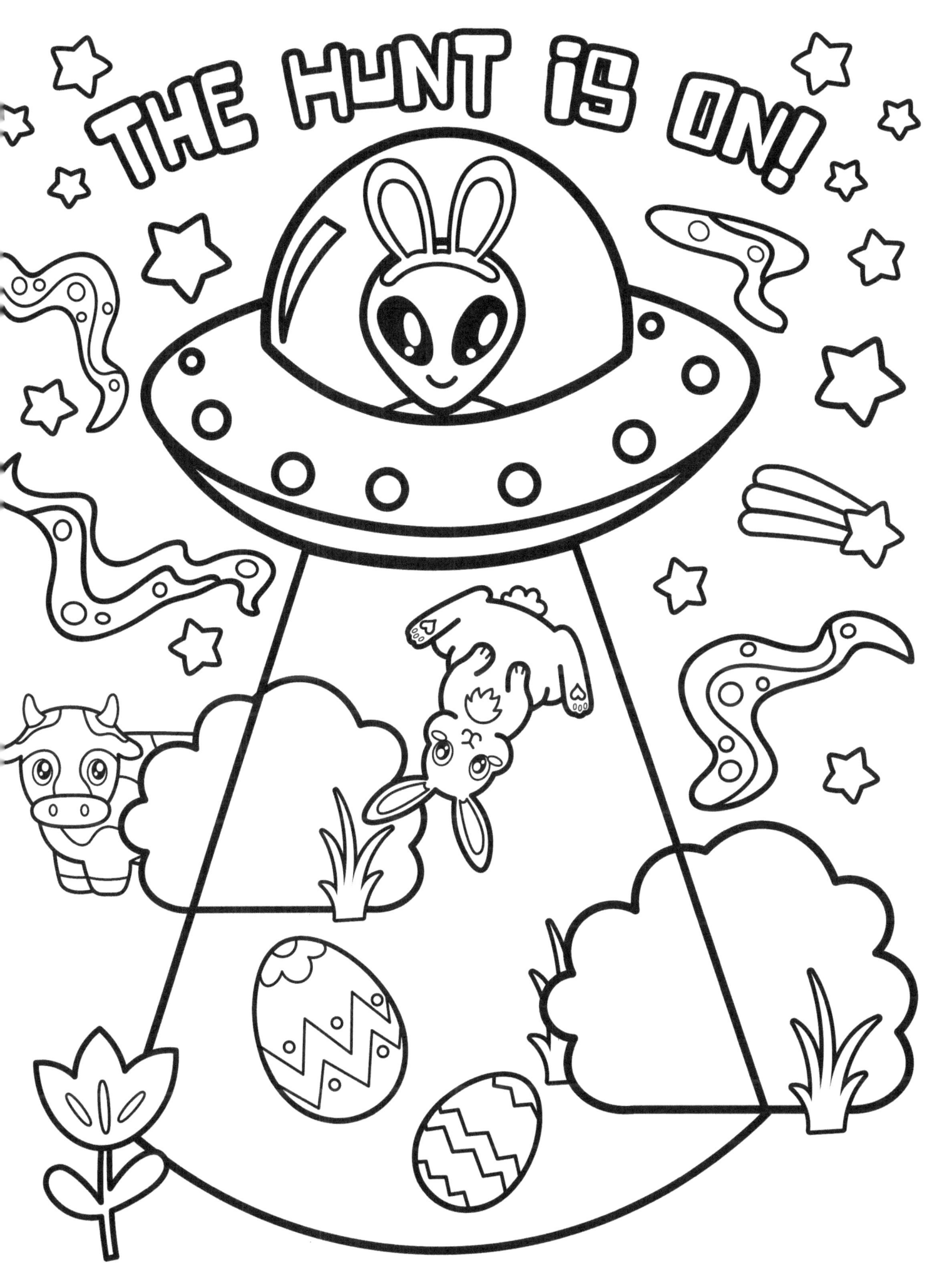

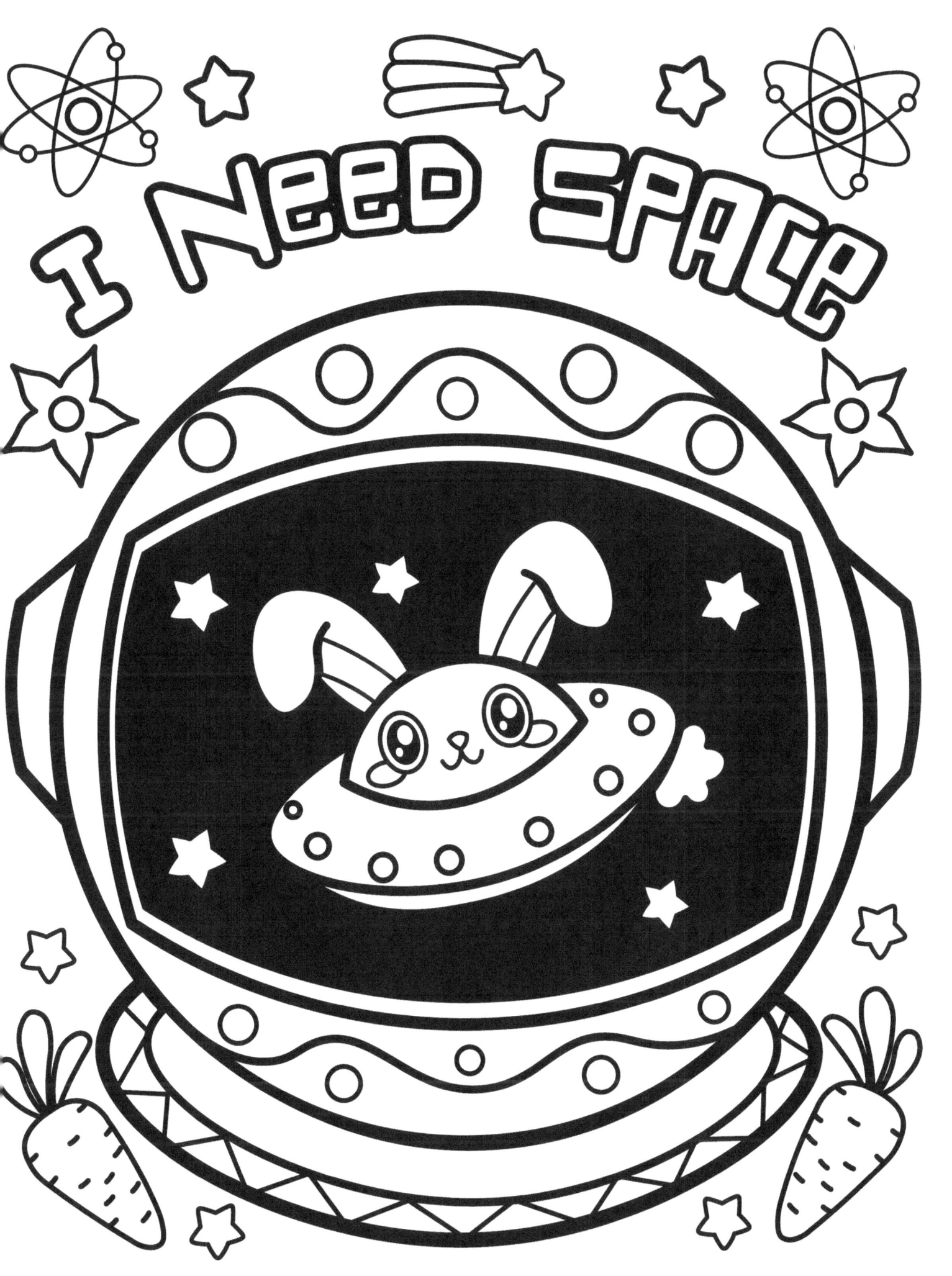

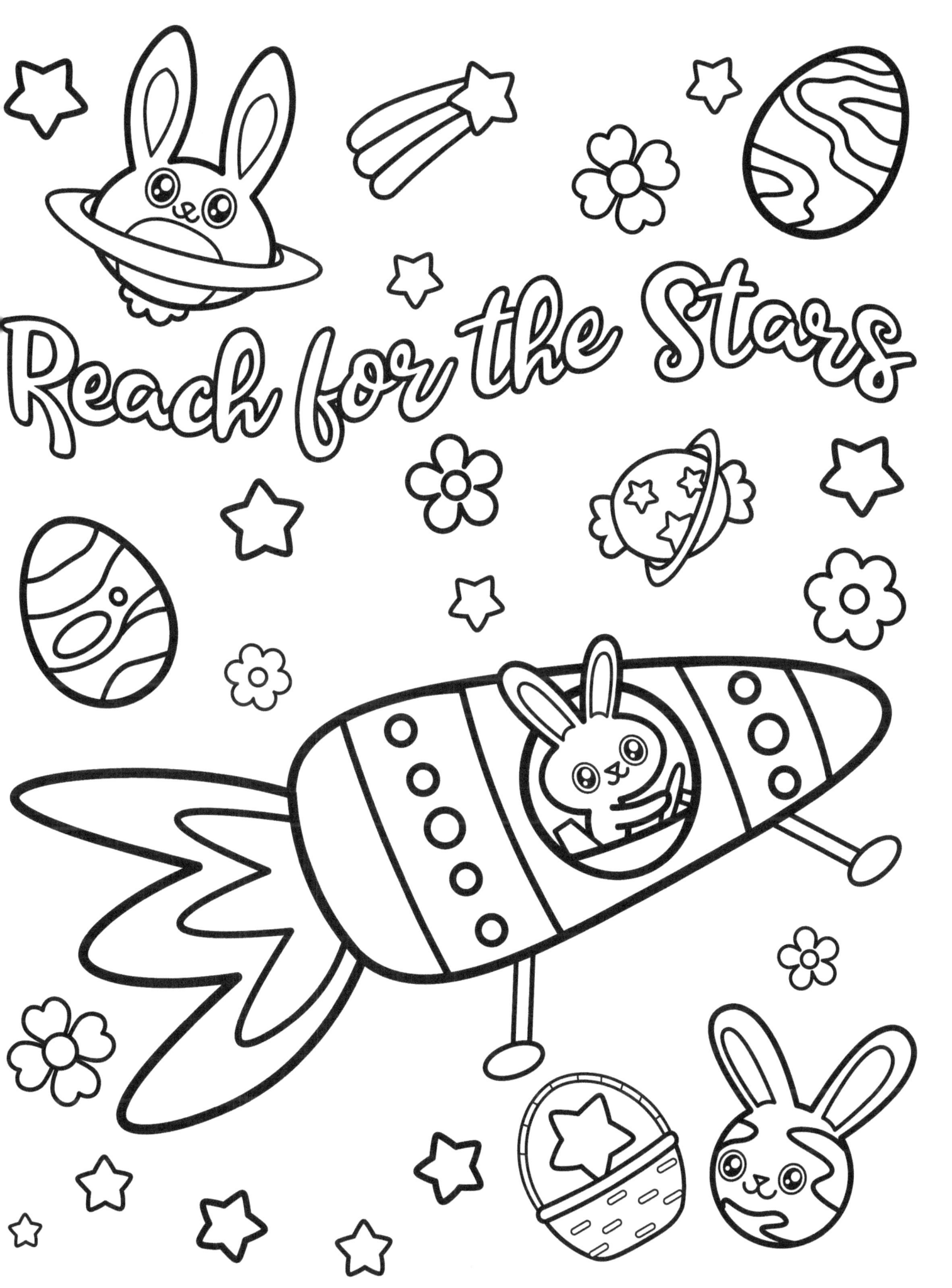

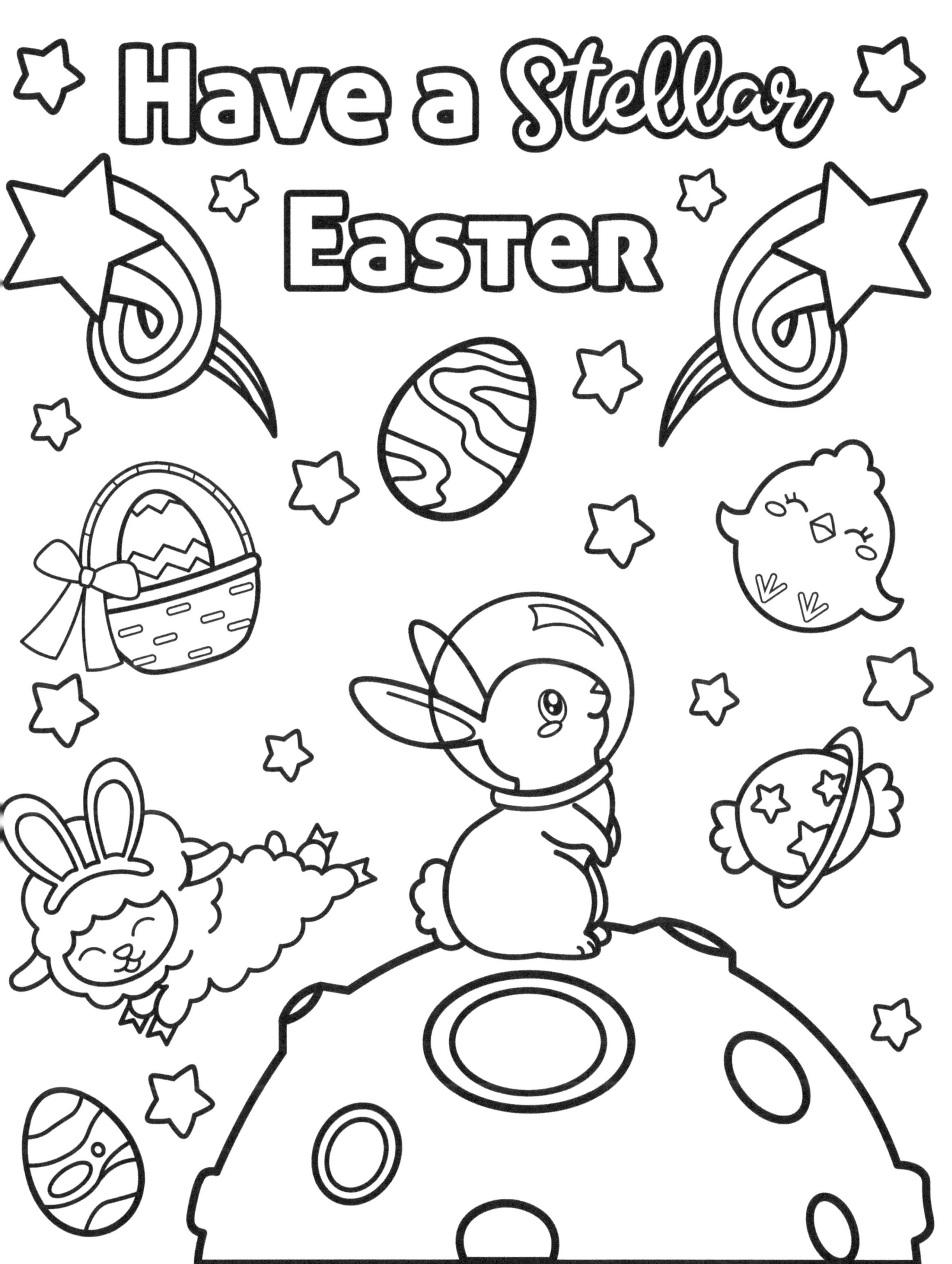

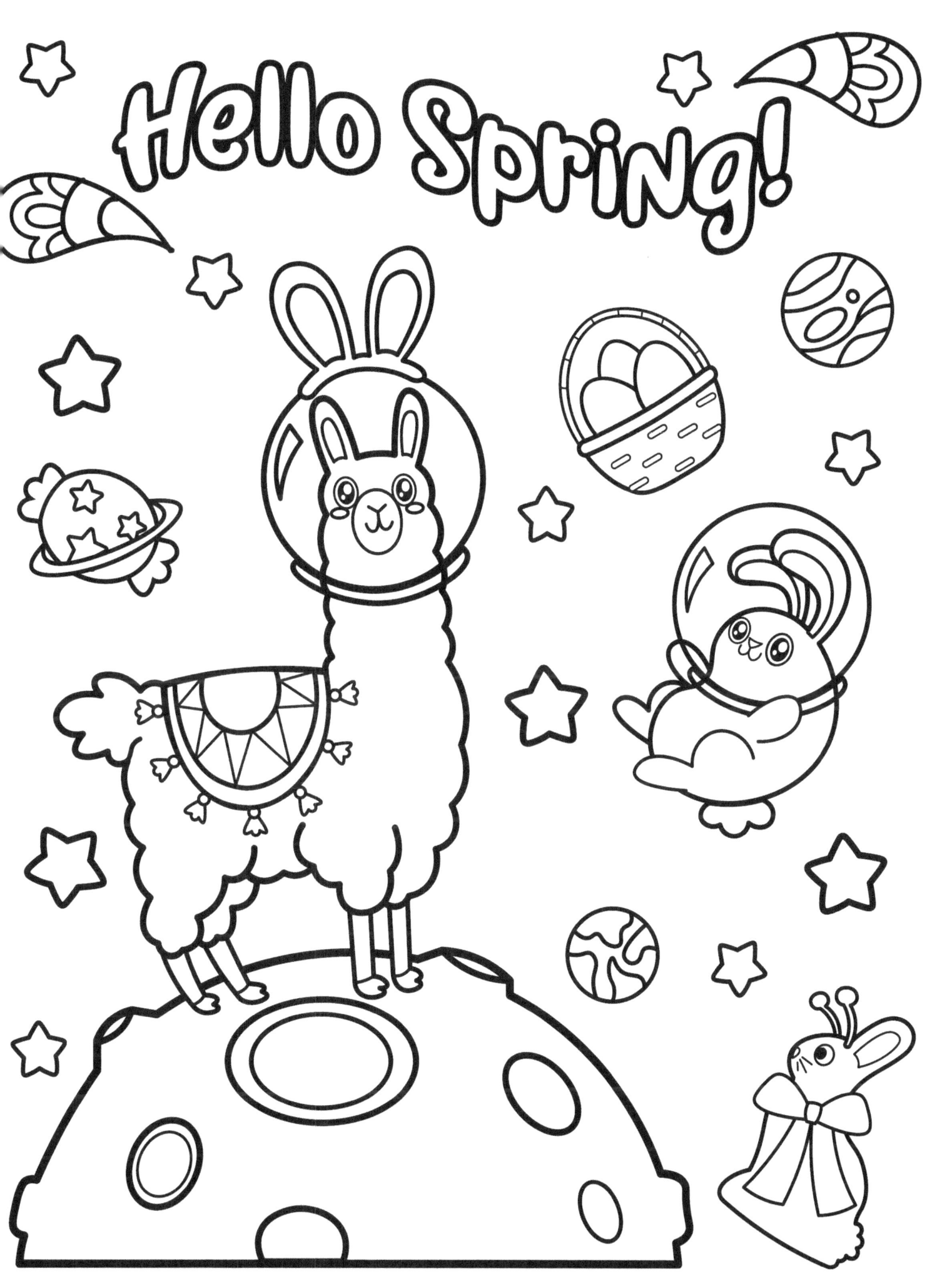

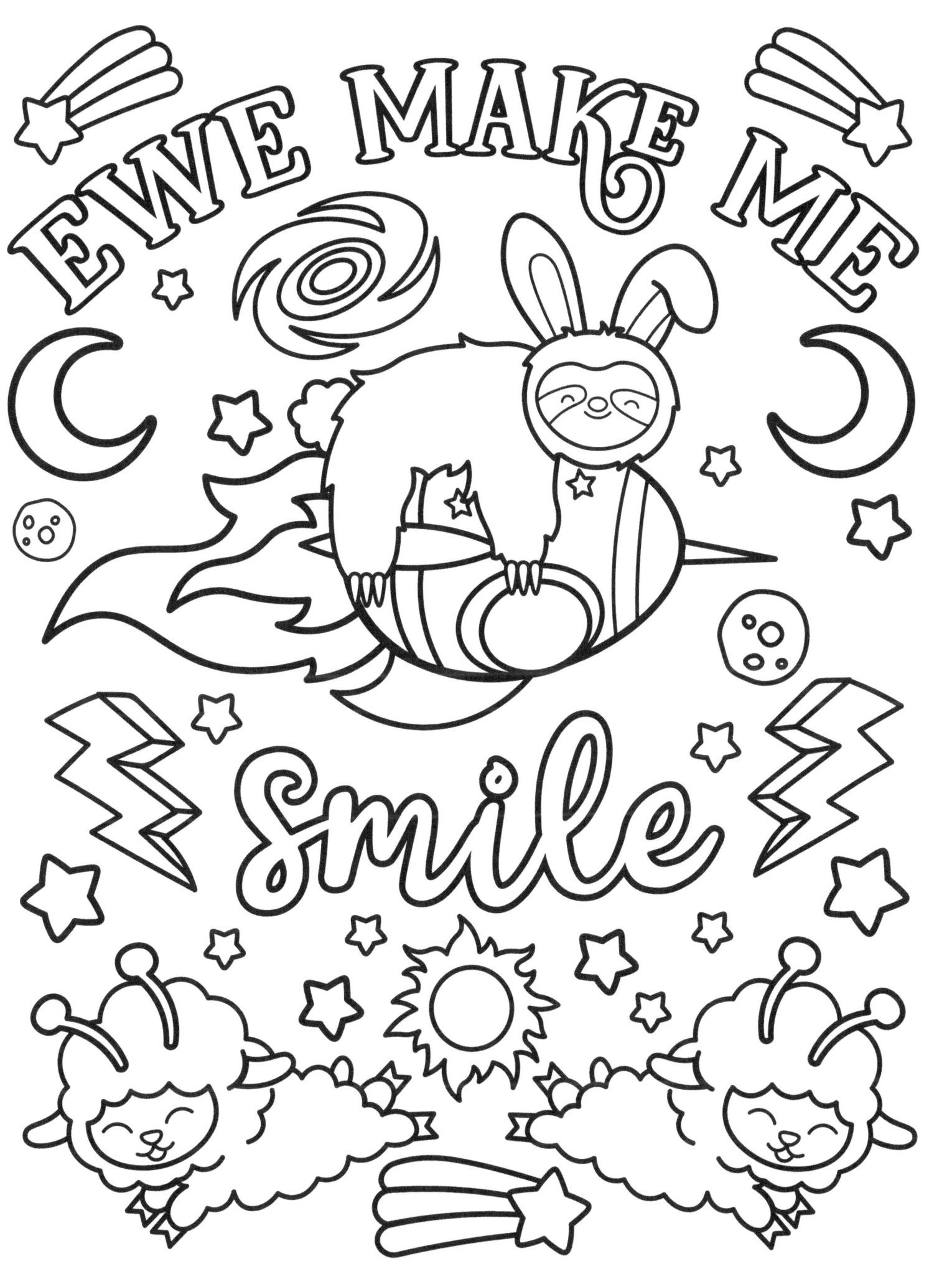

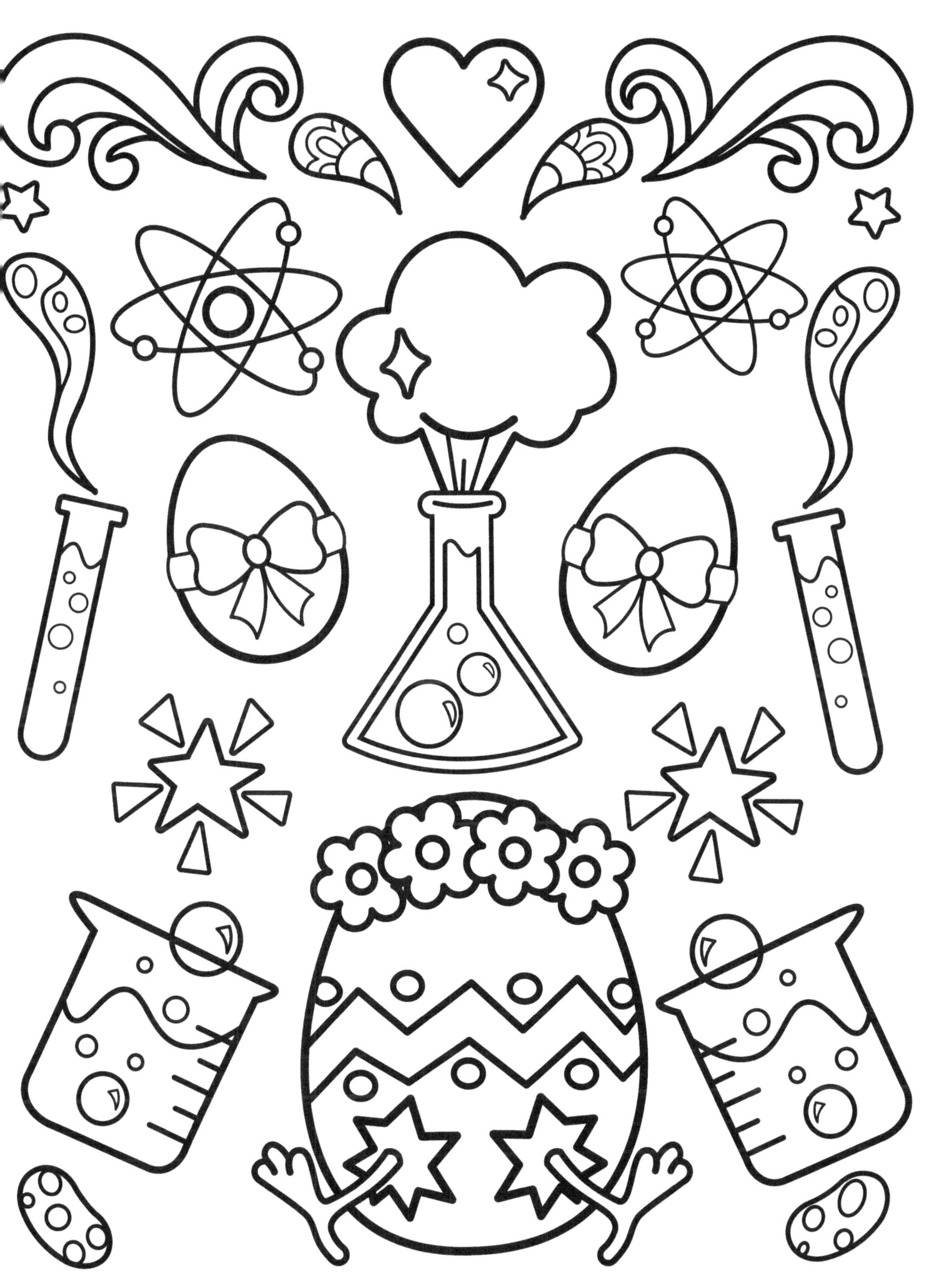

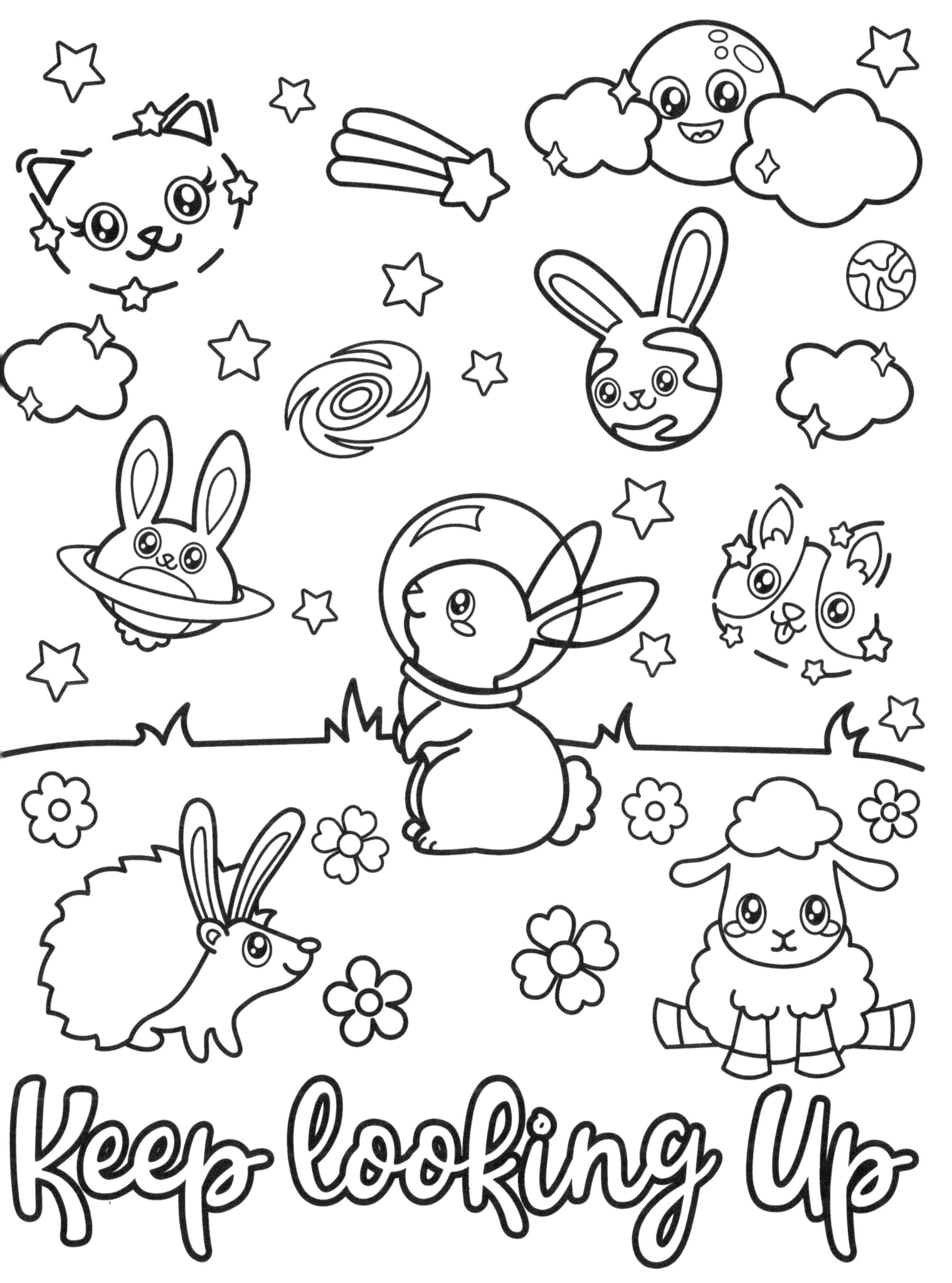

Keep looking Up

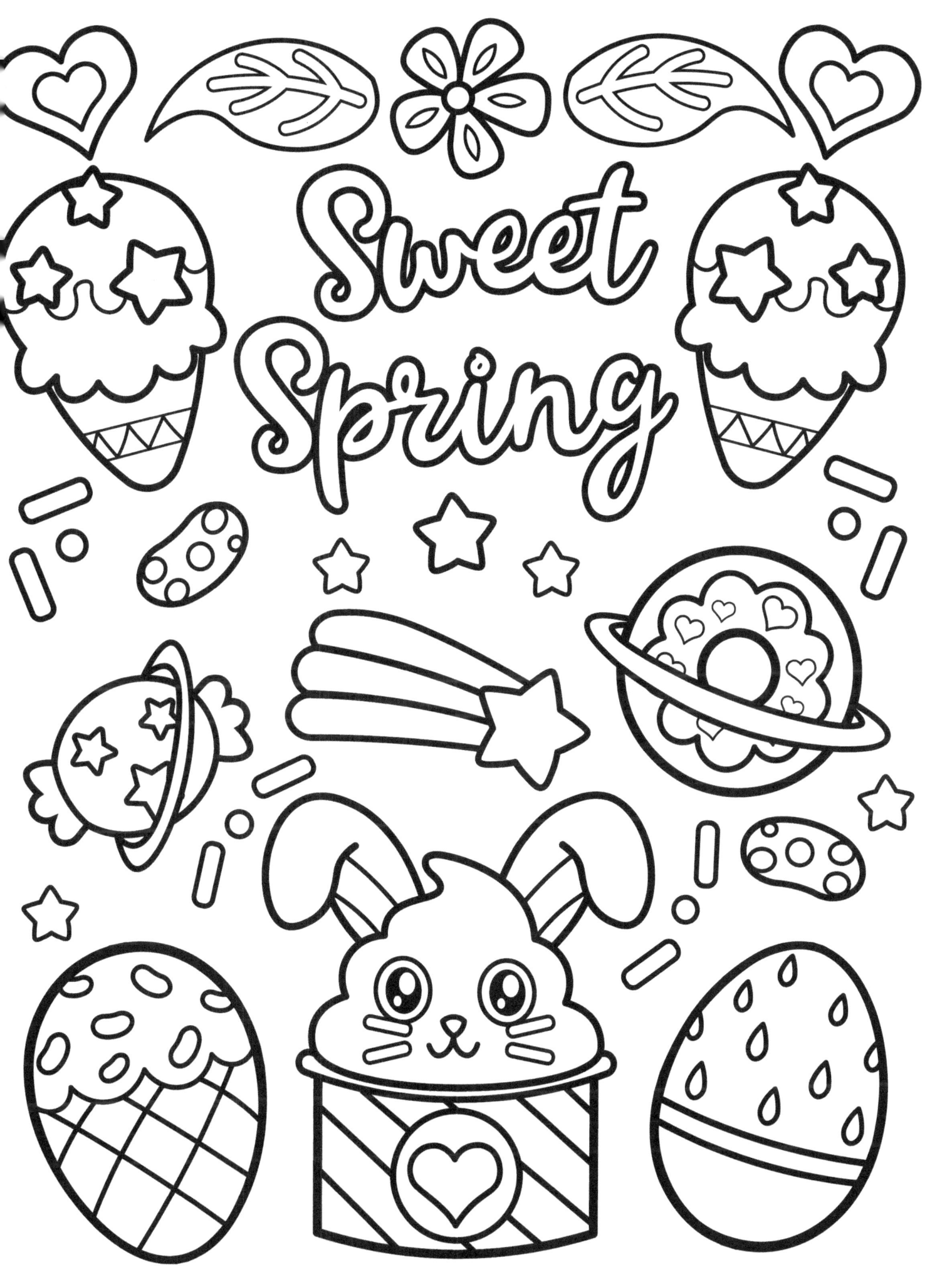

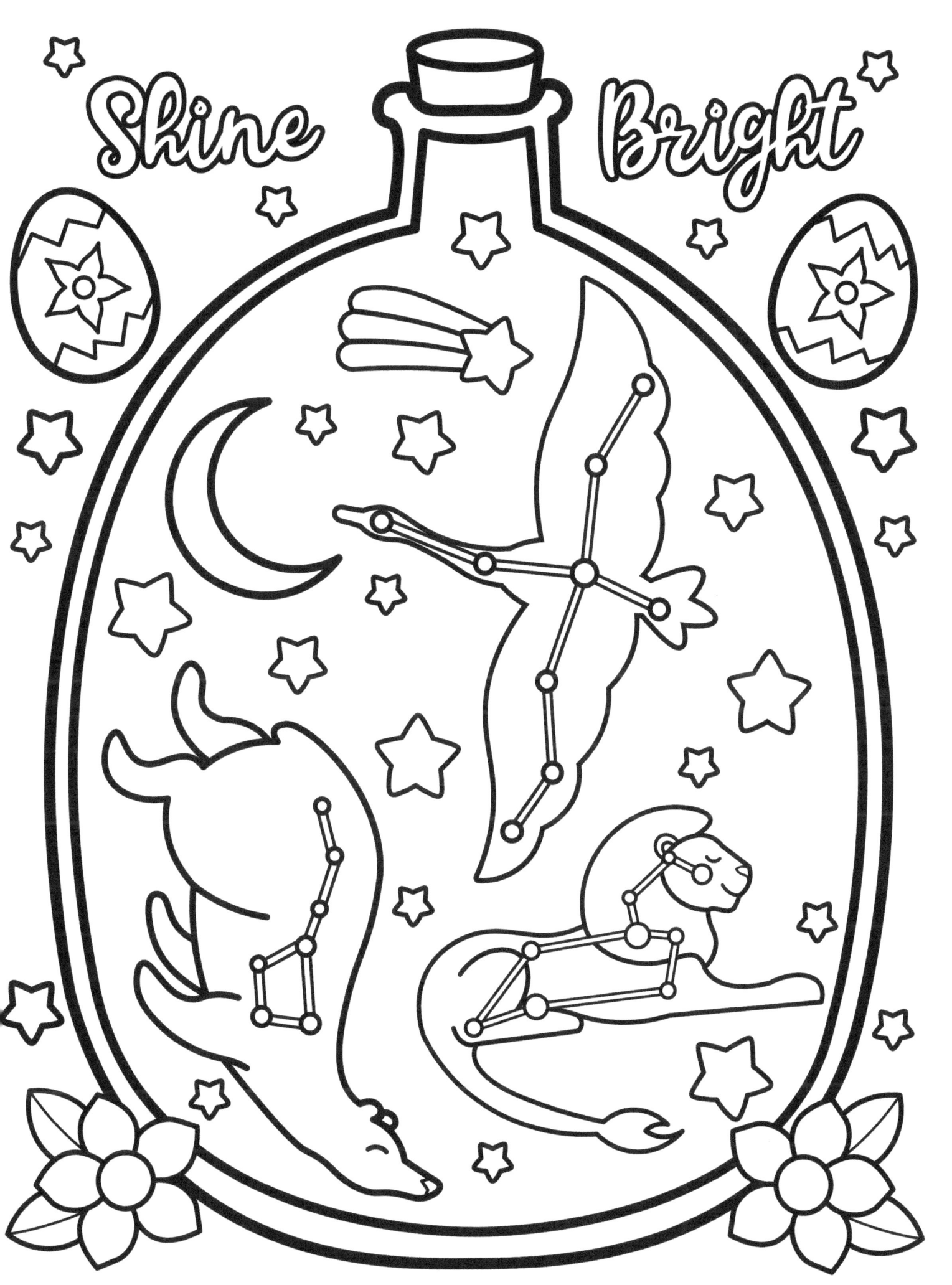

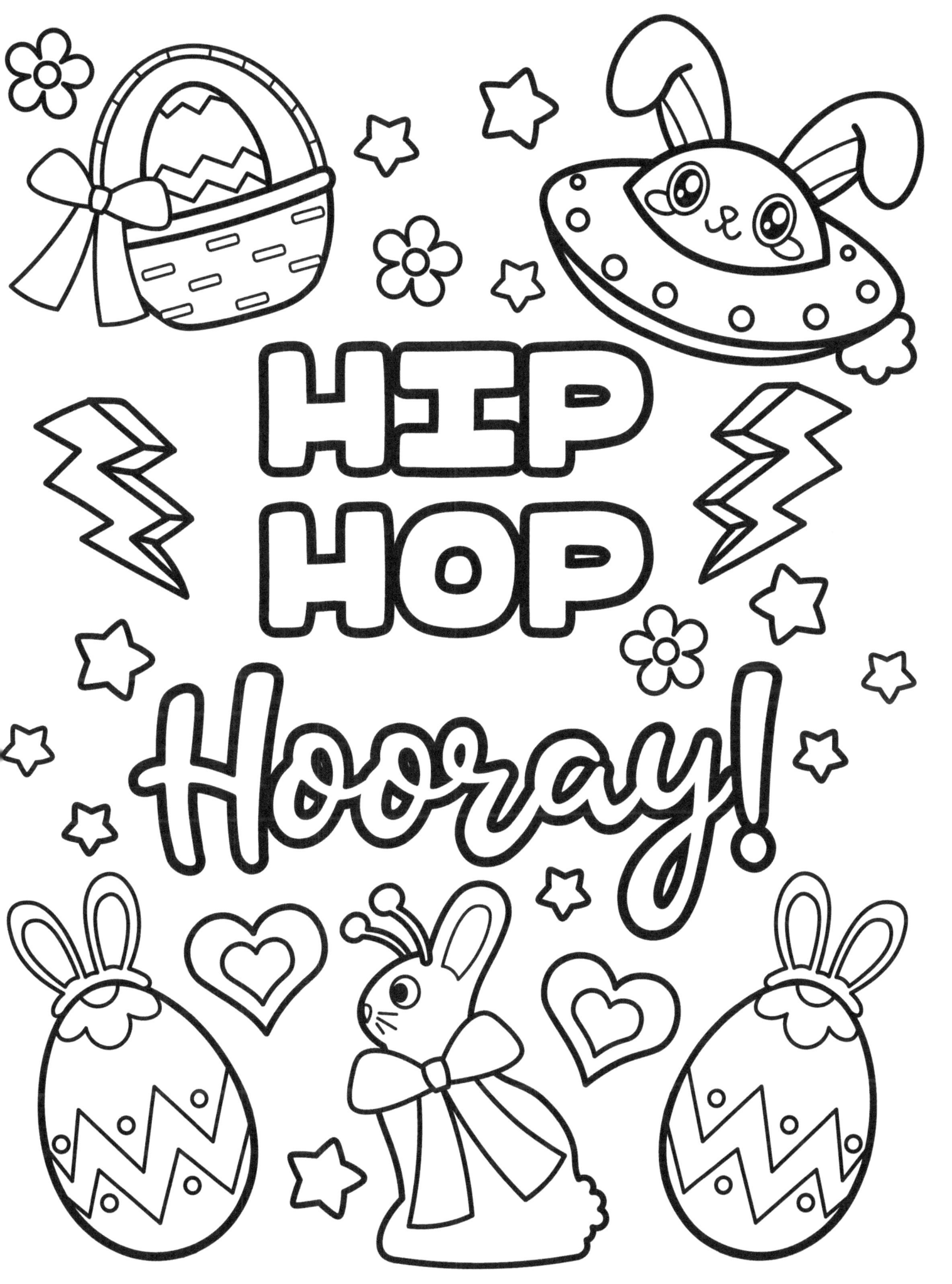

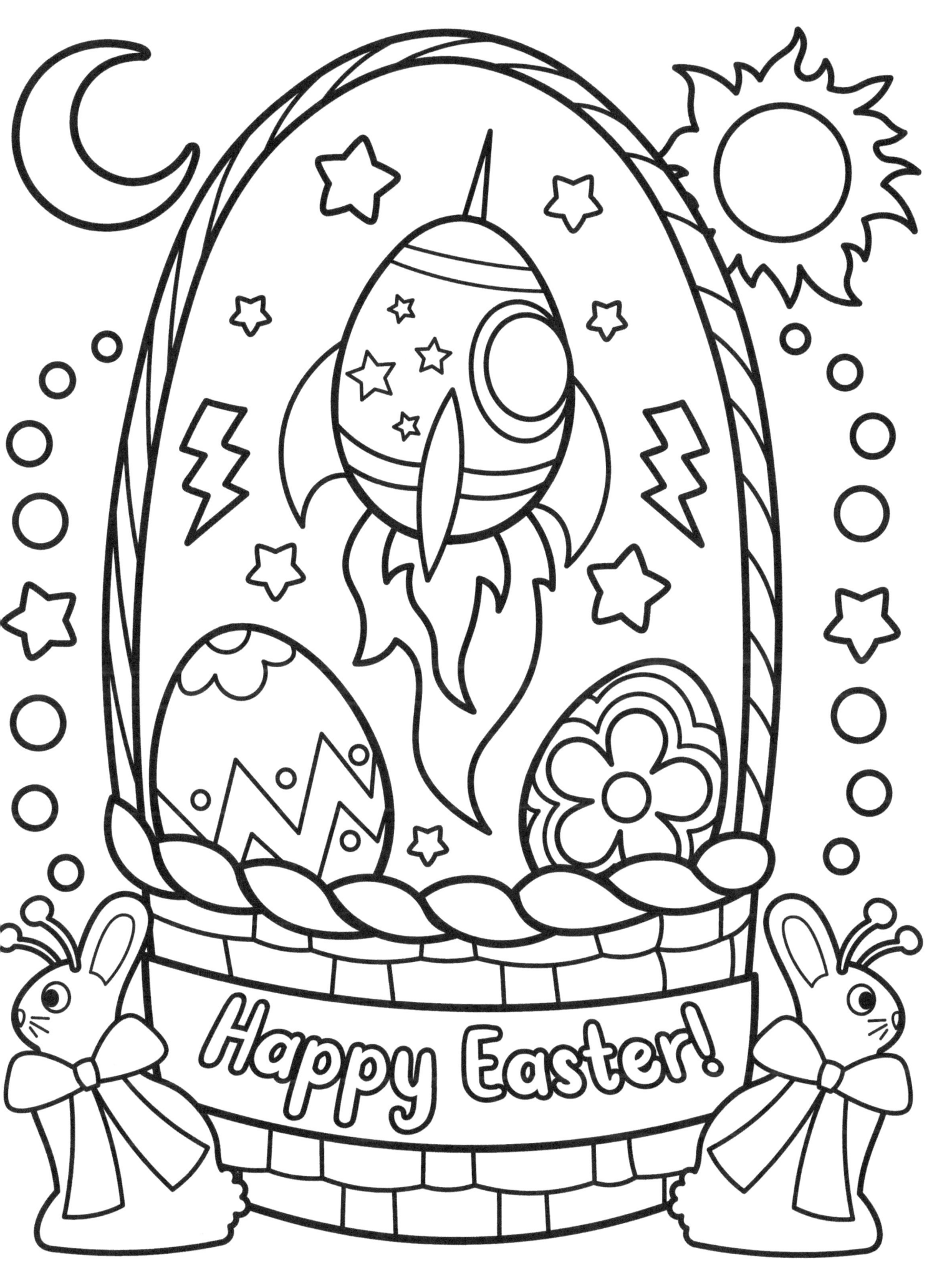

Happy Easter!

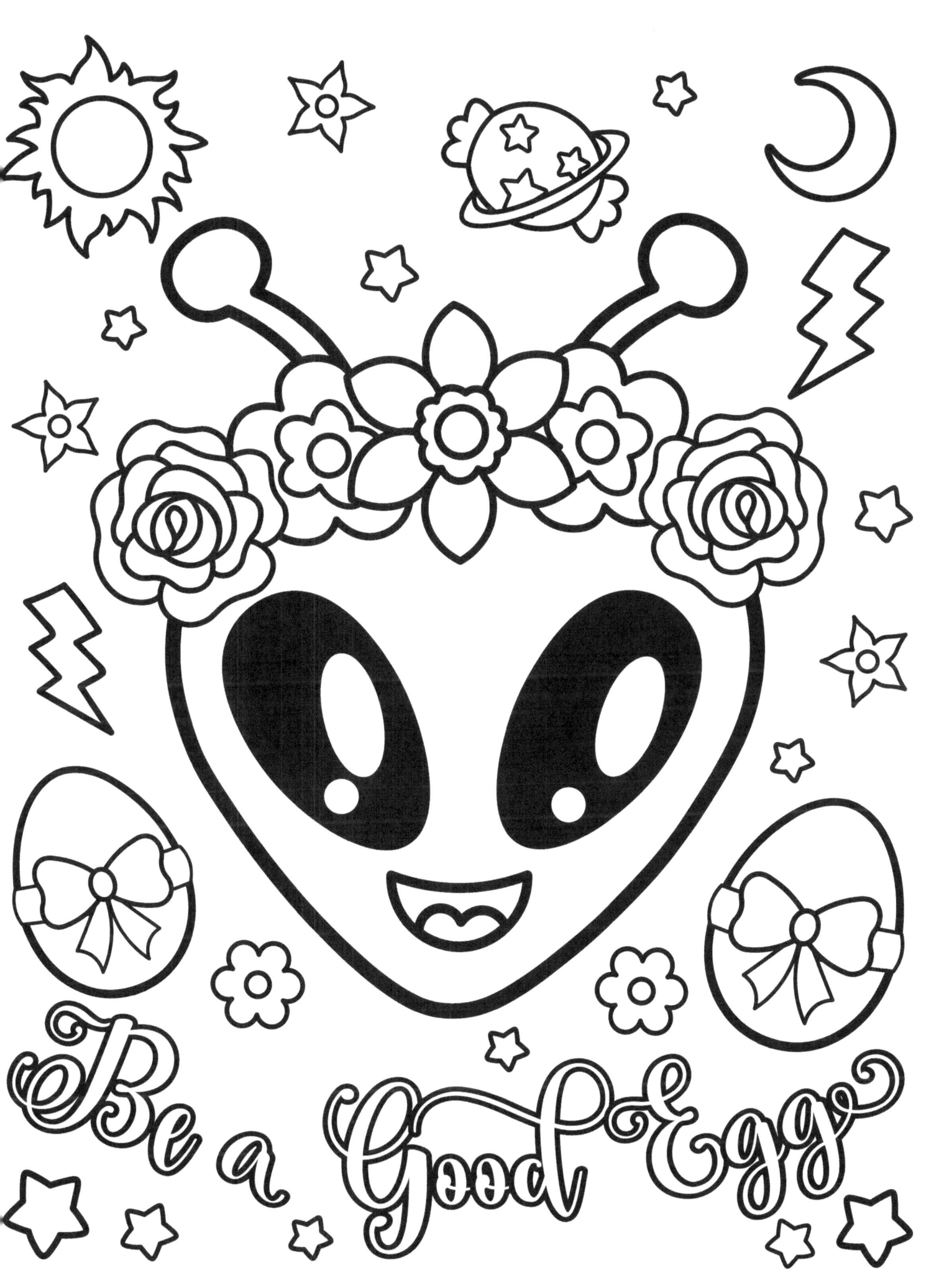

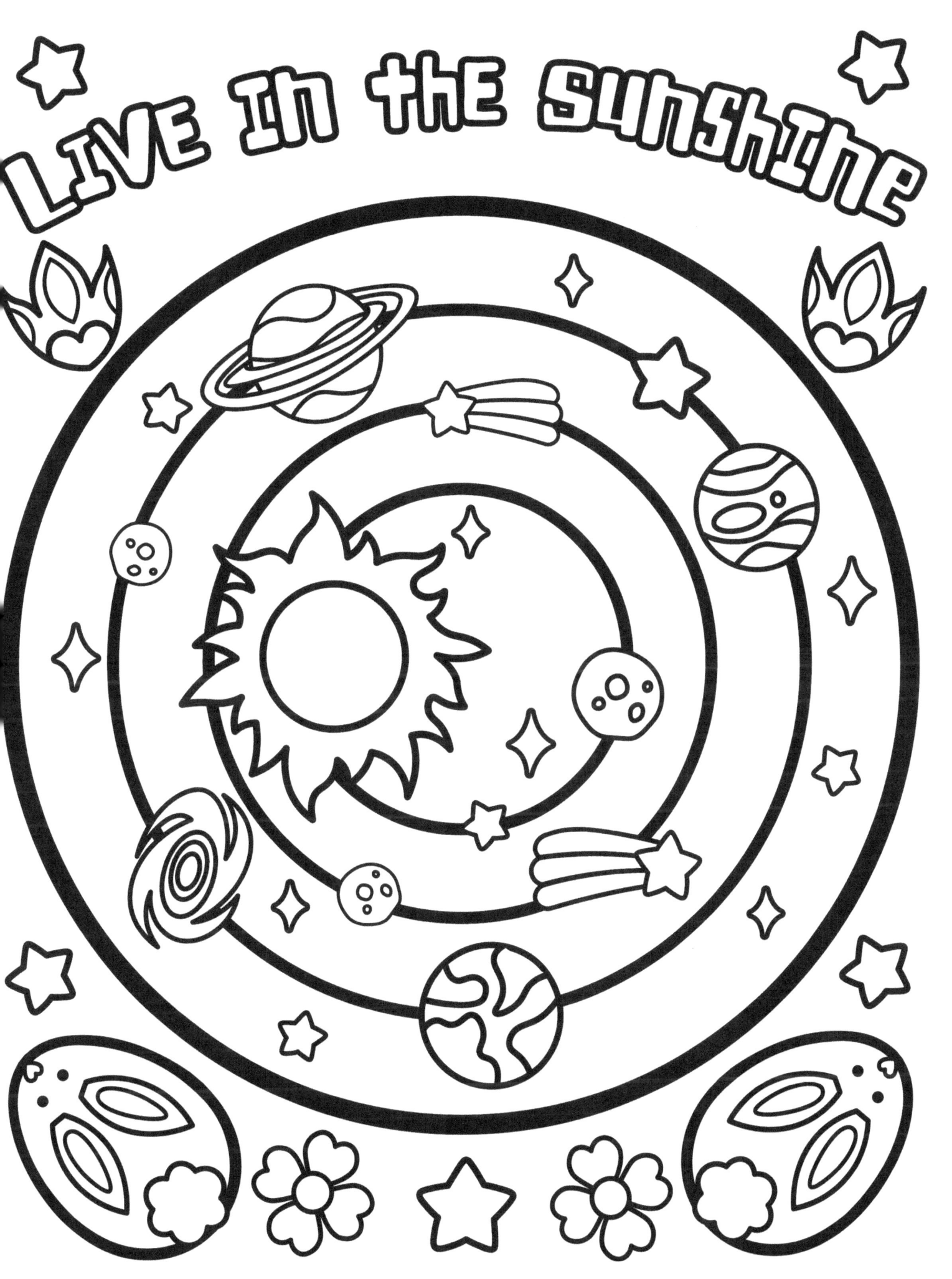

spring Vibes

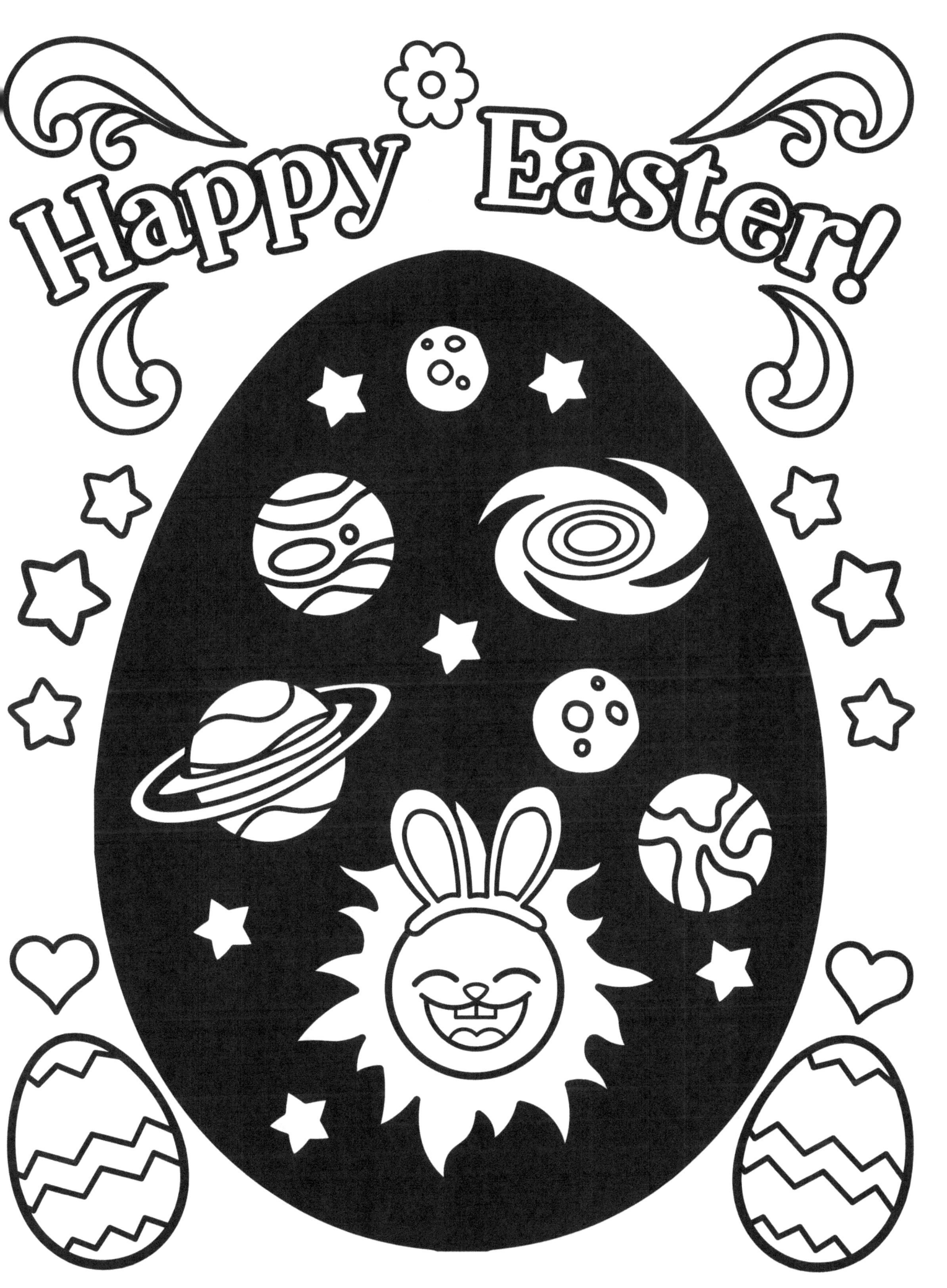

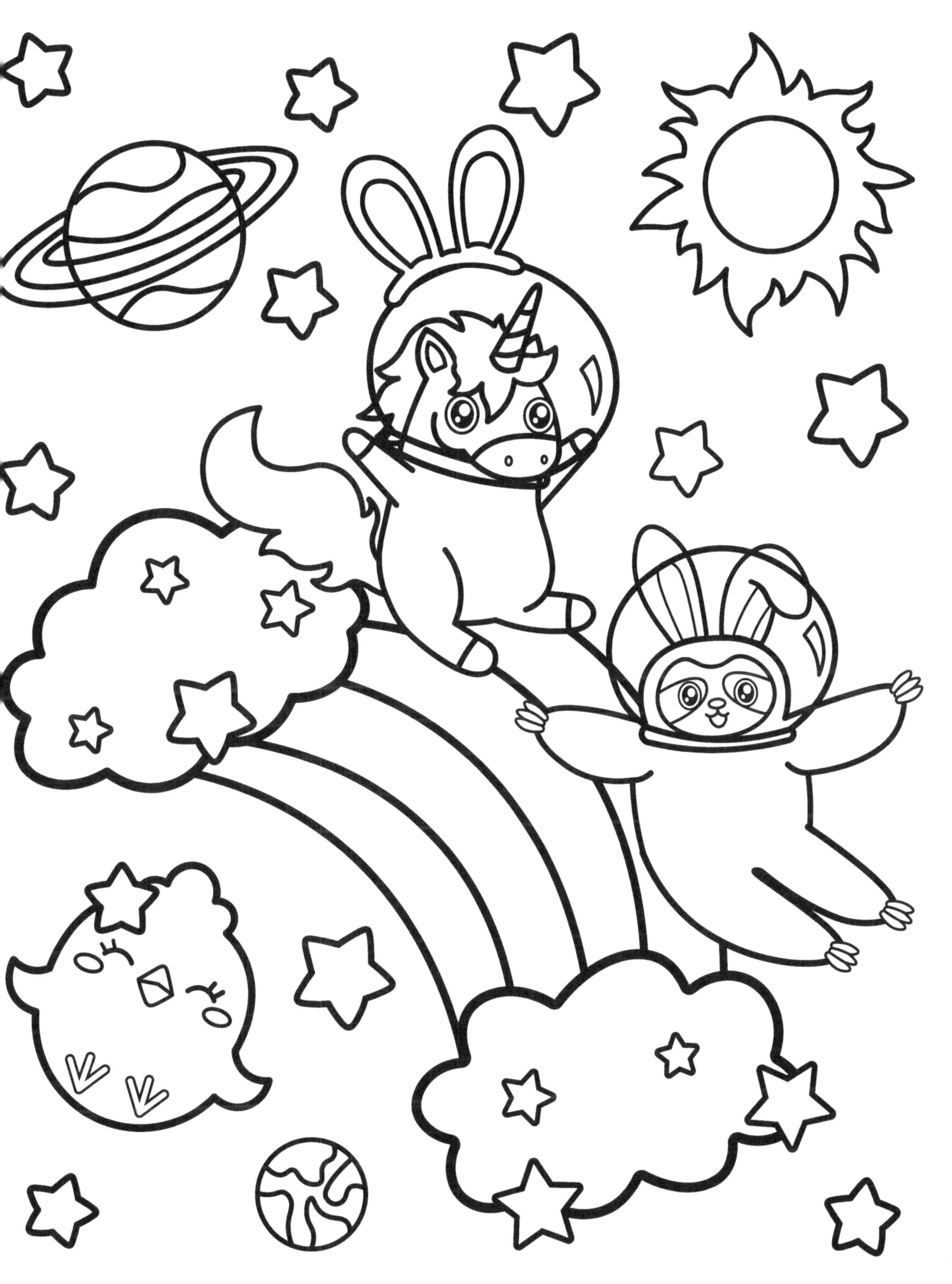

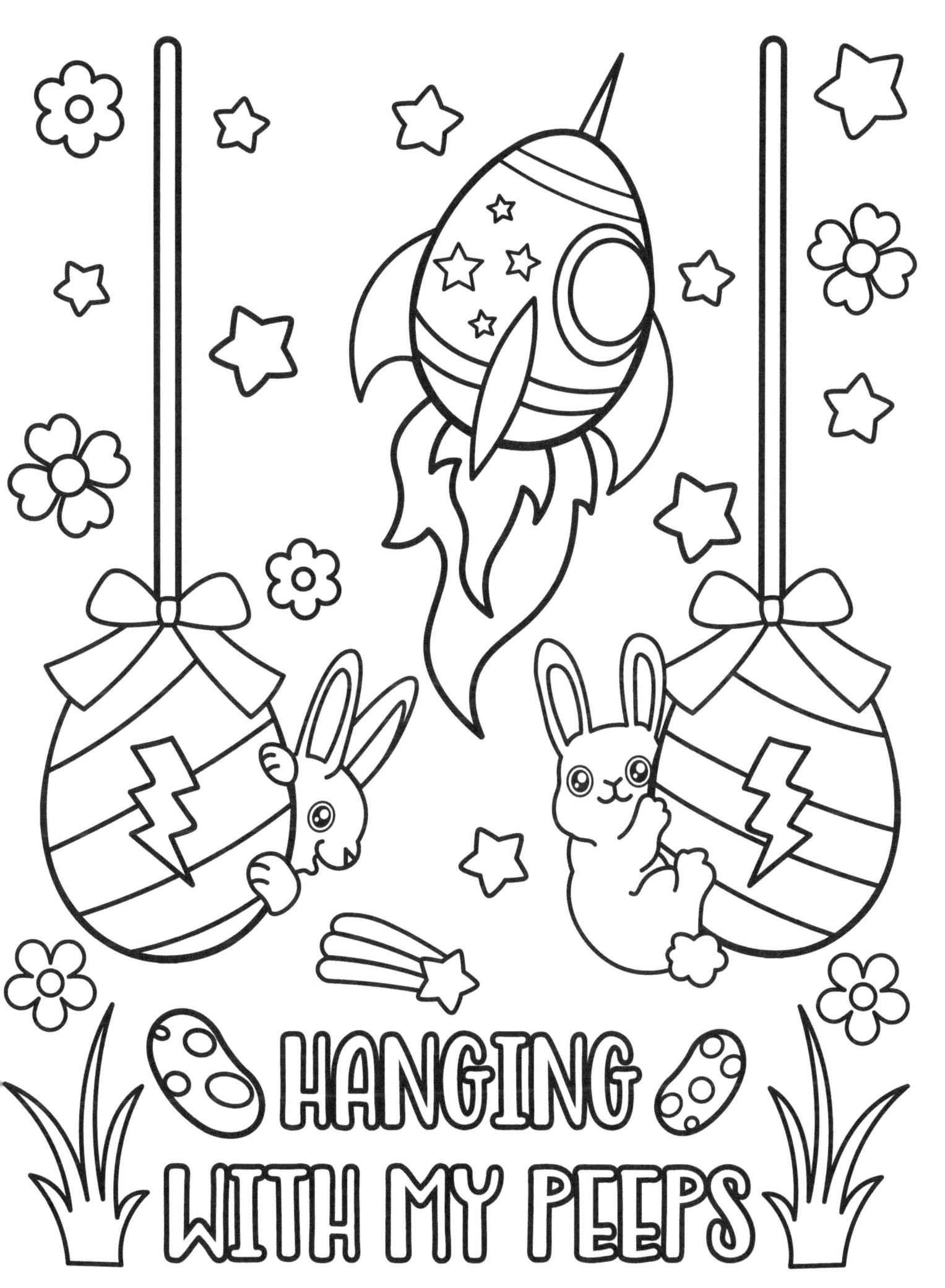

HANGING WITH MY PEEPS

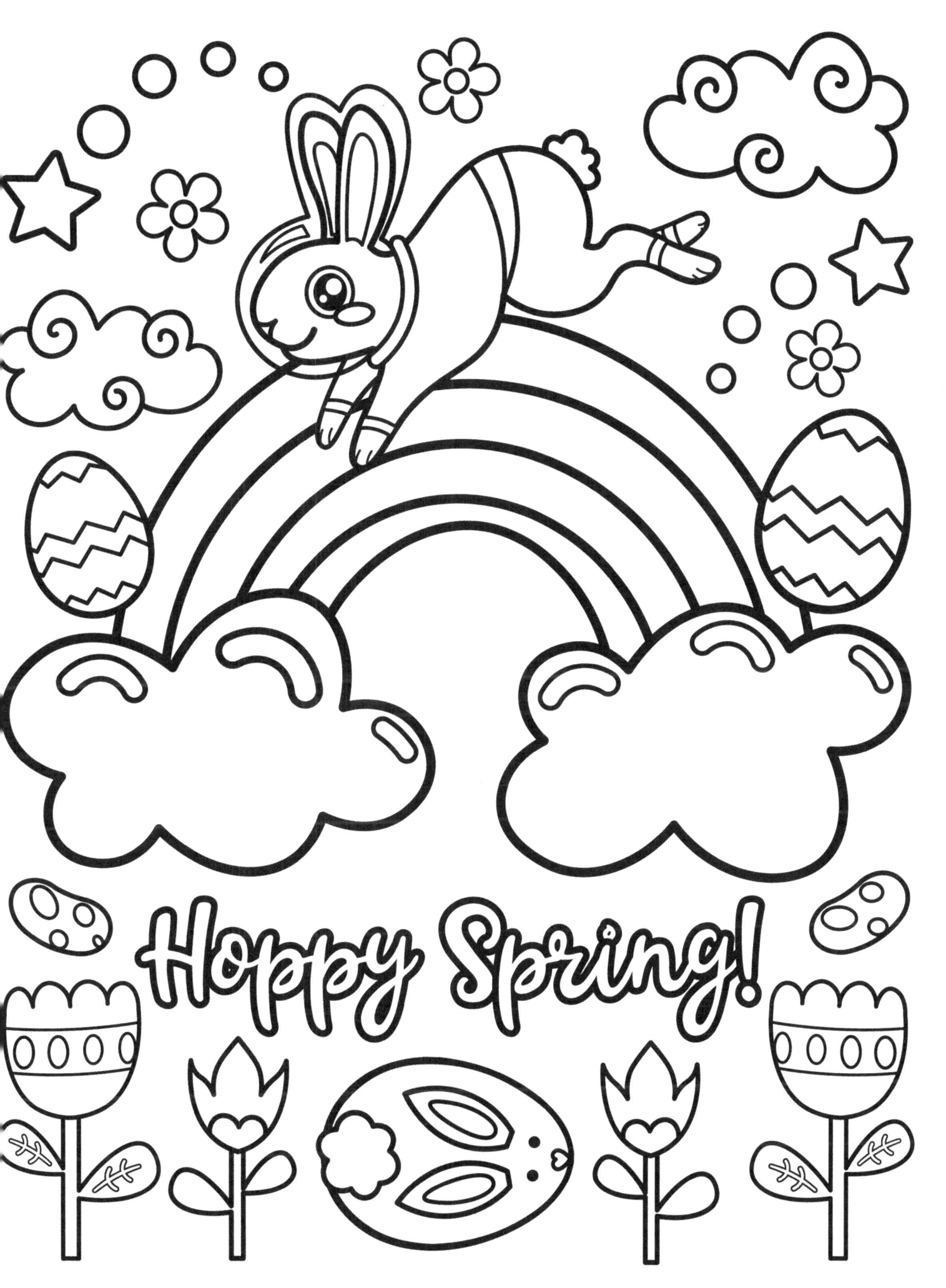

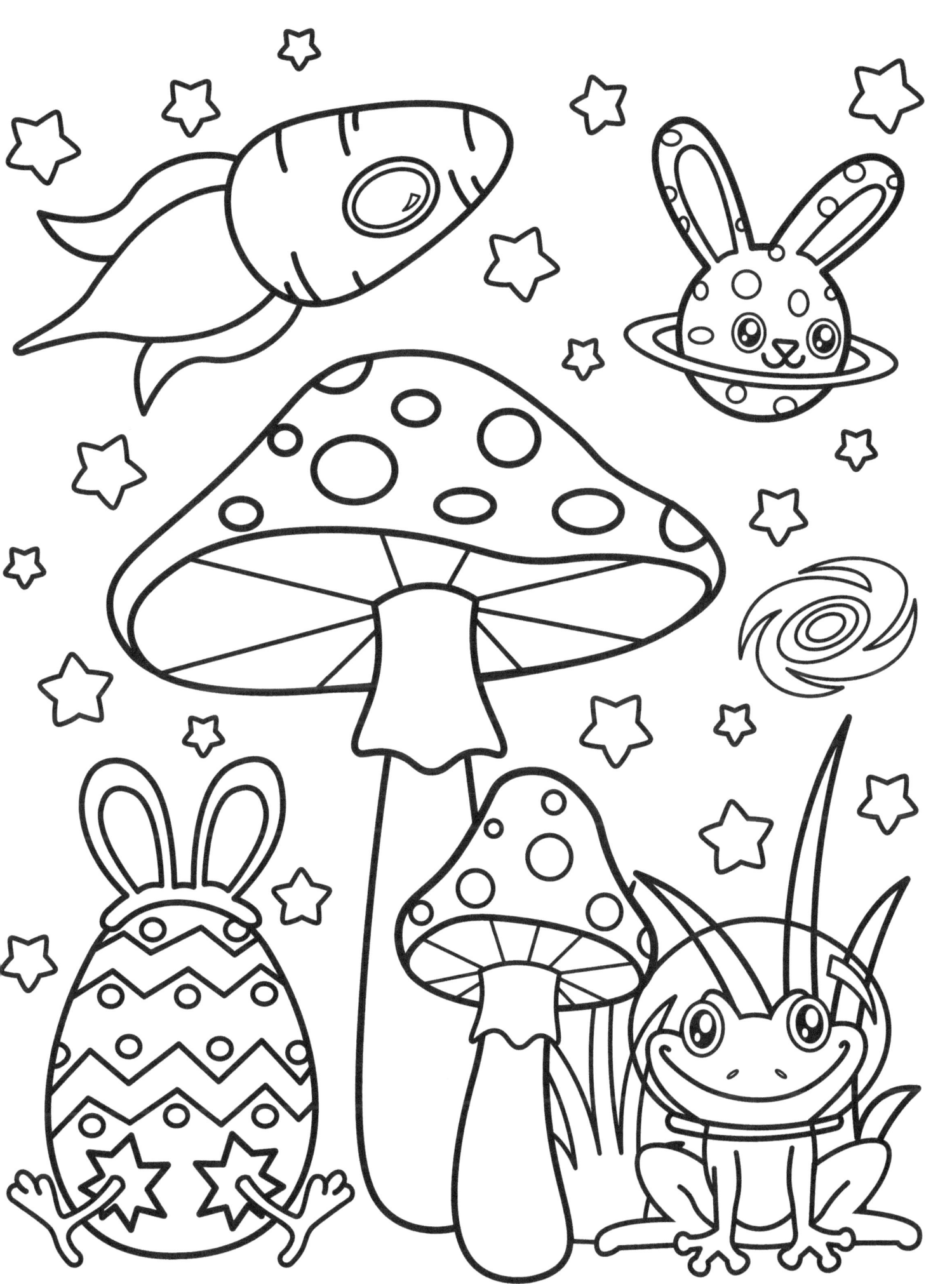

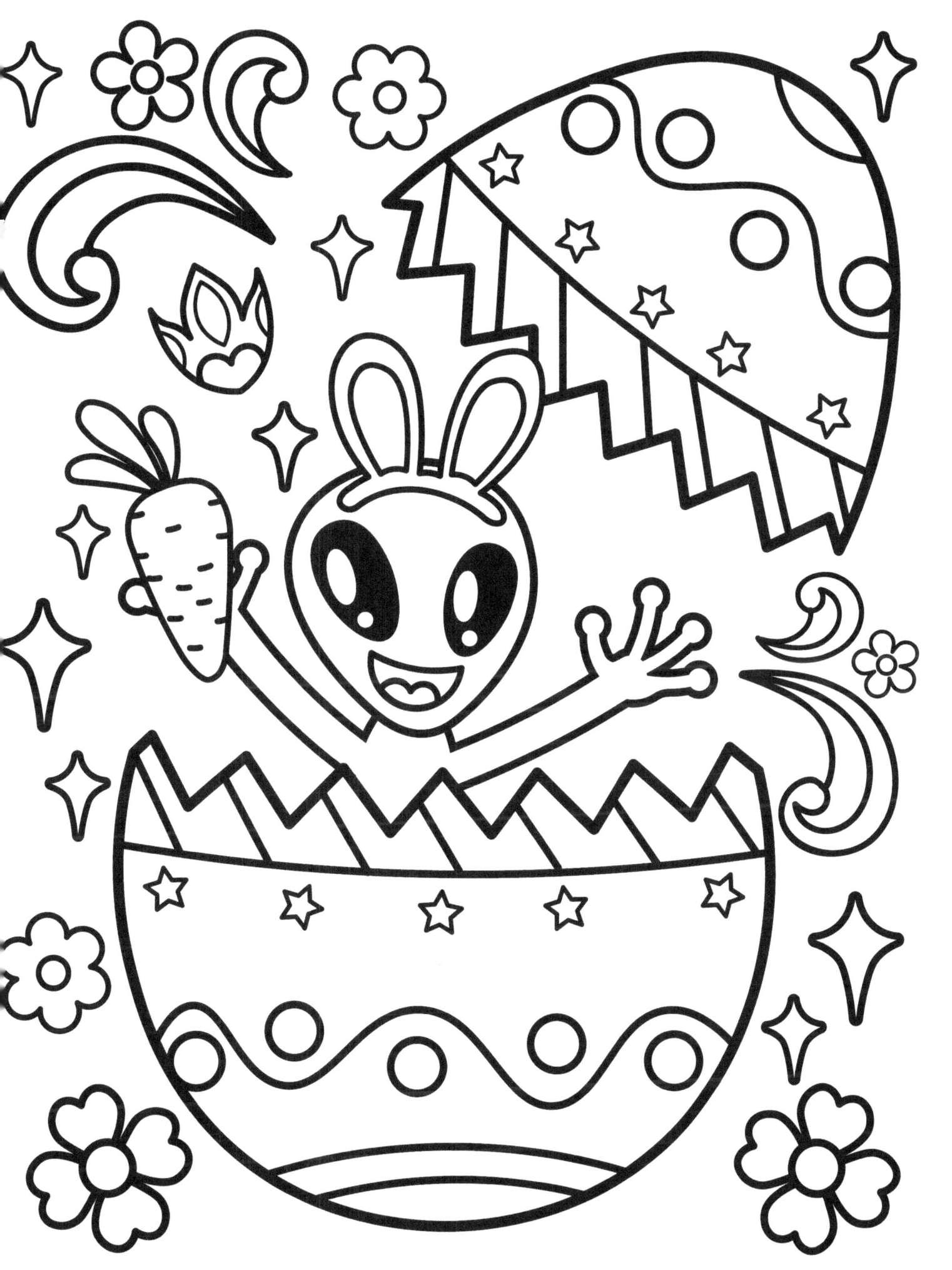

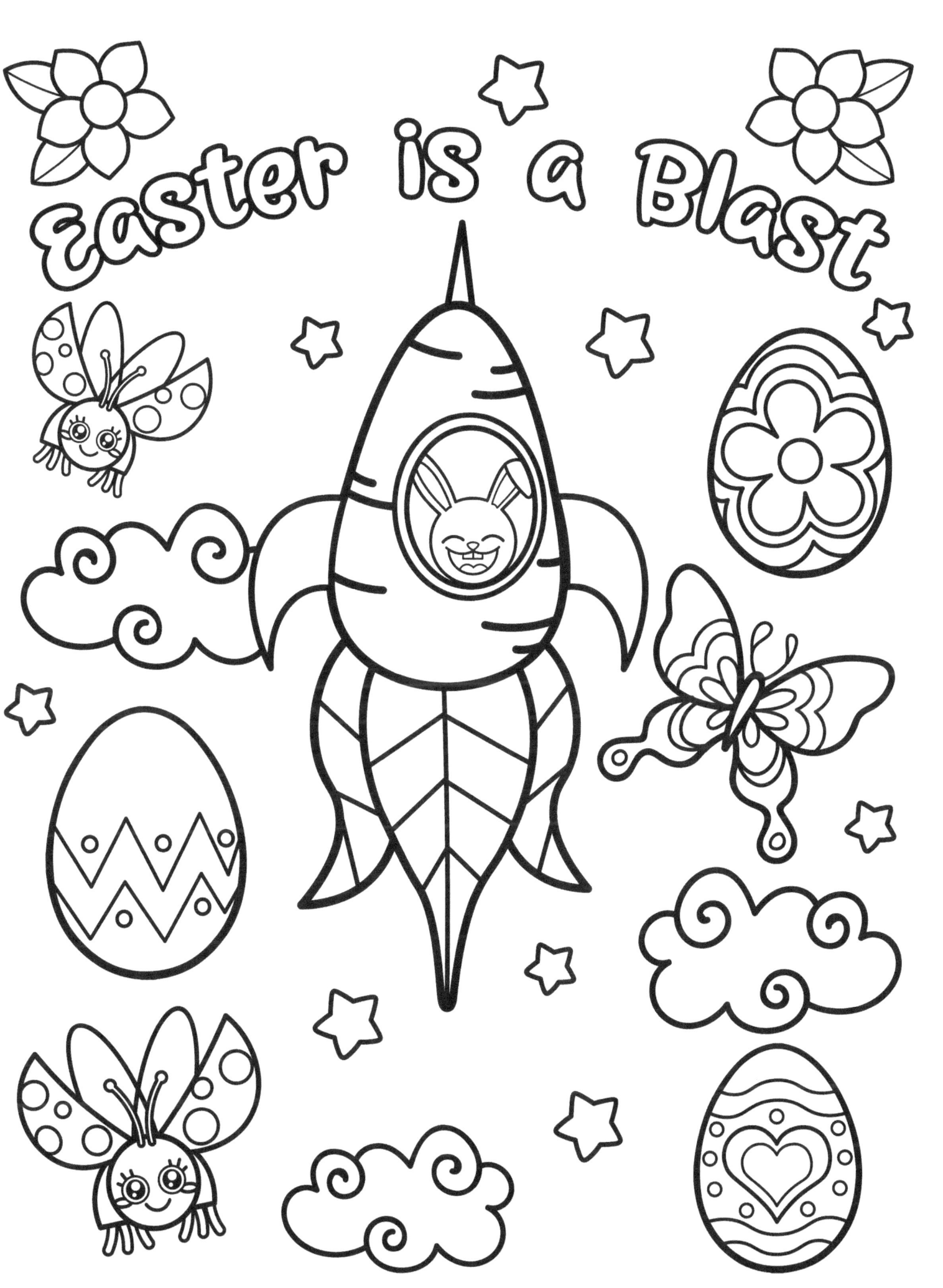

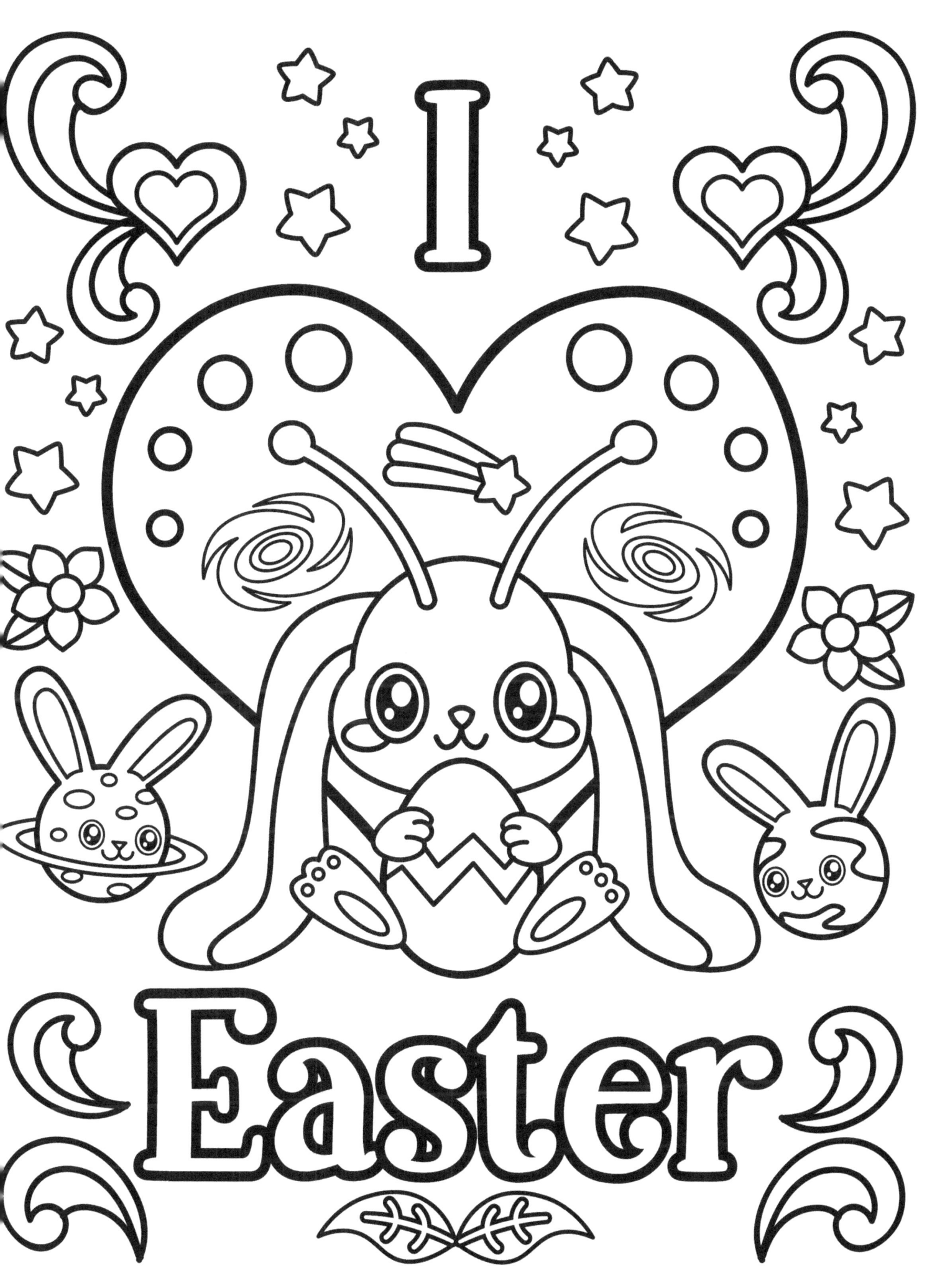

Also by Nyx Spectrum:

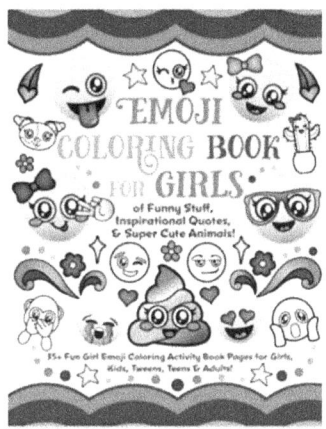 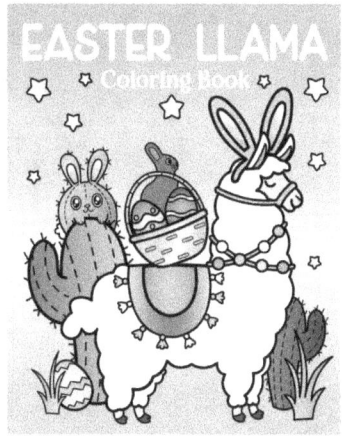 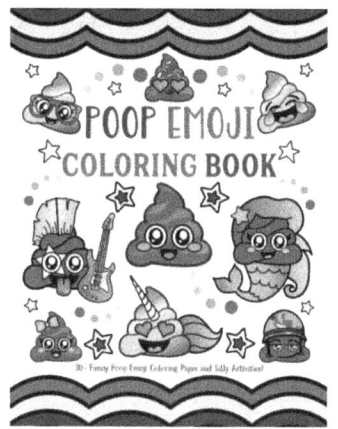 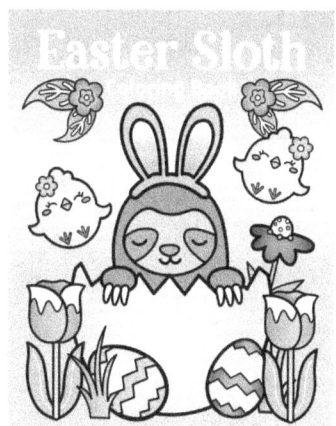

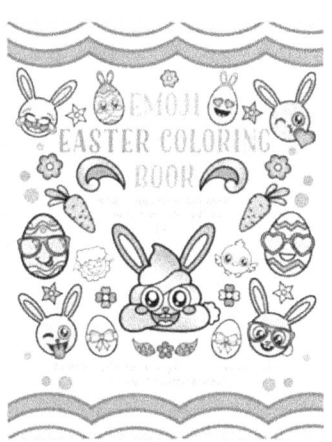 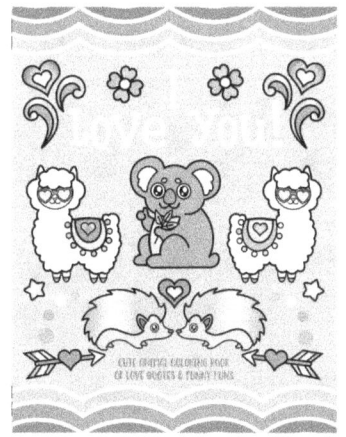 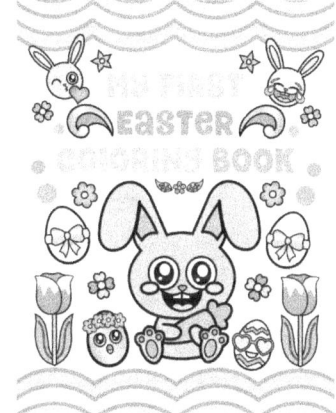 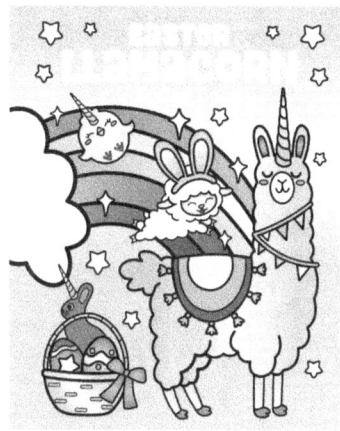

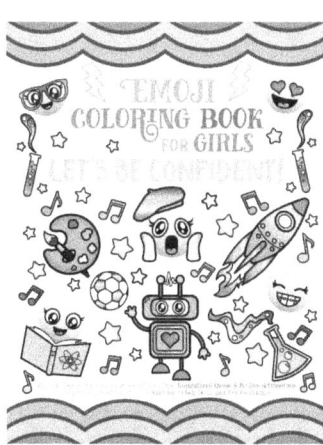 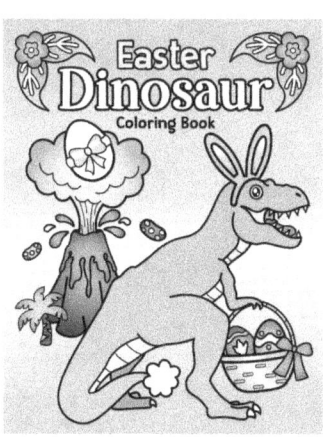 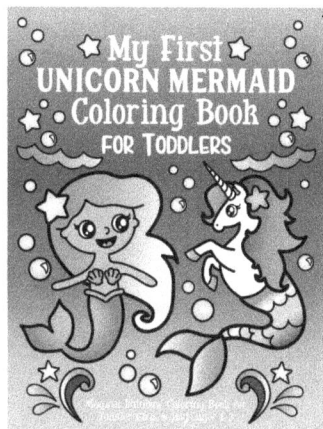 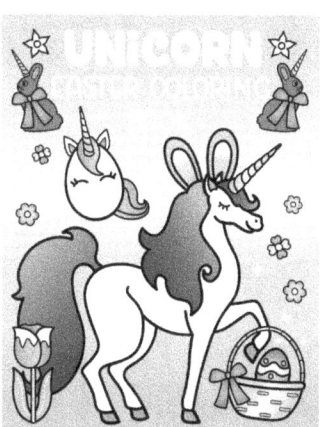

To receive Free exclusive Coloring Pages and future release updates,
please visit us at NyxSpectrum.com and subscribe to our email.
Our books are found only at Amazon.com